As we see Ourselves:

Jewish Women in Nursing

Evelyn Rose Benson, RN, MPH

Center Nursing Publishing

Publishing Director: Jeff Burnham
Book Acquisitions Editor: Fay L. Bower, RN, DNSc, FAAN
Graphic Designer: Michelle Coy
Copy editor: Estelle Beaumont, RN, PhD
Proofreader: Linda Canter
Copyright© 2001 by Center Nursing Publishing

Printed in the United States of America
Composition by Center Nursing Publishing
Printing/binding by Printing Partners
Cover illustration, "Biblical Midwives" by Carla Golembe

Sigma Theta Tau International Honor Society of Nursing
Center Nursing Publishing
550 West North Street
Indianapolis, Indiana 46202
www.nursingsociety.org

ISBN: 1-930538-05-7

01 02 03 04/987654321

As we see Ourselves

Dedicated to

Rebecca, Arthur, Hannah, Elana, Adin
Miriam, Jon-Jay, Gilah, Tsvi, Tova
and to the nurses who shared their stories

and

In memory of Morton

$\mathcal{P}$reface

At the close of the 20th century, society's preoccupation with cultural diversity created a heightened awareness of ethnic identity. People everywhere displayed a growing interest in exploring their personal roots and in identifying the achievements of their ethnic groups. Nurses, like members of other disciplines, began to recognize and acknowledge the contribution of various ethnic groups to the development of their profession. Within this framework it is now timely and appropriate to have a new look at nursing from a Jewish perspective.

Traditionally, nurse-historians have characterized the origins of nursing as an expression of Christian love and charity offered by women in their role as nurturers. In many works on nursing history, the role of Jewish women has been largely overlooked. Furthermore, within the Jewish community, and within the general community, nurses have never enjoyed a fraction of the *koved* (i.e., respect and honor) given to physicians. Nor has nursing, traditionally, been accorded the same status as the other so-called women's professions, such as teaching or social work. In pursuit of their goals, Jewish women in nursing have had to confront and overcome these and other barriers that have been fueled by myths, stereotypes, misconceptions, and lack of information. In recent years, Jewish nurses have begun to respond to the need to set the record straight.

To put it another way, women's history has been excluded from general history and from Jewish history. Furthermore, nursing history has been excluded from women's history, and Jewish women have been excluded from nursing history. The purpose of this book is to fill a gap in nursing history, in women's history, and in Jewish history by identifying the Jewish presence in nursing and by describing the contribution of Jewish women to the nursing profession. As such, this work is addressed to several audiences.

First, the book should be of interest to all nurses who value their heritage, especially in view of the growing commitment of nursing to acknowledge the contribution of diverse ethnic groups to the profession. This book should be of interest, also, to those who study women's history and the role of Jewish women in history. Historically, nursing developed as a woman's profession, although in recent years a concerted effort has been made to recruit men. In examining the development of nursing, we must look at the role of women in society throughout the ages for a better understanding of how the nursing profession evolved. Finally, this book is addressed not only to nurses and to students of women's history, but also to members of the community at large and to members of the Jewish community, all of whom are actual or potential consumers of nursing service.

Writing this book has been a challenge and has helped to cement old friendships and create new ones. I owe a debt of gratitude to Nira Bartal, a nurse-historian from Jerusalem, who gently but persistently moved me back on track with my work. My deepest thanks go to Sylvia Firschein, Jewish librarian and storyteller par excellence, who provided me with wonderful resource materials. Bertha Rose came through when all others failed. I greatly appreciate the contribution of Dr. Baruch Hurwich, who generously shared his expertise. Dr. Joan Lynaugh and Dr. Karen Buhler-Wilkerson of the Center for the Study of Nursing History at the University of Pennsylvania were very helpful, as were Dr. Zane Wolf, Dean of the School of Nursing, and Mr. Stephen Bredelove, Reference Librarian, of LaSalle University. Other librarians who helped were Judith Leifer of the University of Pennsylvania Judaic Studies Center, as well as Genevieve Berner, Jill Thomas, and Sue Vision of the Haverford Township Free Library. Thanks also to Ann Silverstein of the Beth Ahabah Museum and Archives in Richmond, to Susan Woodland at the Hadassah Archives, and to Dr. John Parascandola, the Public Health Service historian. I am especially grateful to Dr. John Holman, who kept me "in sync" with my computer. I offer special thanks to Betty Solodar, who helped me with Yiddish expressions. I gratefully acknowledge the help of Dr. Fay L. Bower, Dr. Jane Root, and Jeff Burnham who guided the manuscript through the publication process. My dear friend, Alice Lois Gray Smith, and my counselor, Dr. Marsha Dorman, cheered me on. Dr. Ljubica Poleksic shared her expertise. Thanks to Dr. Sharon Beck, Dr. Nettie Birnbach, Dr. Shirley Fondiller, Janice Greenwald, Ruth Grossberg, Rabbi Marshall Maltzman, Rabbi Kenneth Stern, and Rabbi Jon-Jay Tilsen—all of whom read and critiqued various portions of the manuscript. And finally, my thanks and love to Rebecca and Miriam, their spouses and children, who were always there to prop me back up into the vertical when the going got rough.

Contents

Part I: Nursing History Revisited: A Jewish Perspective

Part II: The Jewish Presence in Contemporary Nursing

$\mathcal{P}$art III: Lest We Forget

$\mathfrak{I}$ntroduction

This book is divided into three parts: I. A discussion of nursing history from a Jewish perspective II. A description of the Jewish presence in contemporary nursing III. A review of Jewish nurses in wartime service

This work attempts to create an awareness of the Jewish presence in a field that has been historically identified by its "Christian" tradition. In tracing the history of nursing and in exploring the Jewish contribution, one must recognize that these topics cannot be examined in isolation. They must be viewed within the context of the historical role of women in society.

Part I—Nursing History Revisited: A Jewish Perspective

This section begins with a historical overview of nursing in the quest to document the role of Jewish women. Modern secular nursing is a very young profession, but *nursing,* as a universal response to human needs, is as old as the human race. Accordingly, Chapter 1 goes back to Biblical and Talmudic texts in search of nursing roots through references to women and to their role as nurturers and caregivers. It shows that, in fact, the Jewish heritage in nursing can be traced back to ancient times.

Chapter 2 explores the "Middle Period" of Jewish history from the post-Talmudic era into the 18th century. Reference is made to Jewish communal efforts in caring for the sick throughout the long history of the Jewish people. Chapter 3 captures the dawning of a new era for Jews, women, and nursing. We enter the modern period of nursing by reviewing the Nightingale legacy and the nursing reforms that followed.

Chapter 4 traces the progress of nursing in early 20th century America and shows how young Jewish immigrant women were encouraged to enter the nursing profession. The Jewish community and Jewish women of the early 20th century contributed to the continued growth and development of the nursing profession and to many other related health, social, and welfare movements. Chapter 5 identifies several Jewish women from the first half of the 20th century who added luster to the nursing profession. By and large, these women or their parents came from Central or Eastern Europe from that generation of Jewish immigrants who, in seeking a better life for themselves and for their children in the United States, enriched the social, scientific, and cultural aspects of their new country.

Part II—The Jewish Presence in Contemporary Nursing

In this section contemporary Jewish women and their experiences in nursing are described. The emergence of ethnicity as a societal issue in late 20th century America had an impact on nursing. Within the ranks of nursing were several ethnic or other special-interest groups, such as Black nurses, Hispanic nurses, Philippine nurses, Christian nurses, and so on. No corresponding coalition of Jewish nurses existed until 1990 when they began to network through nurses councils established within the framework of Hadassah. It was altogether fitting that this connection be forged in this way since Hadassah's roots lie in nursing. Jewish nurses welcomed Hadassah's establishment of the nurses councils, which seek to promote solidarity at home and to provide support to nurses in Israel.

In Chapter 6 there is a description of an attempt to reach out to Jewish women in nursing and to encourage them to share their experiences. Also, an explanation is given about how and why a search for Jewish nurses was launched. The author introduces the findings of an informal survey that resulted from this search.

Chapter 7 elaborates on the histories that were obtained from Jewish nurses who participated in the survey mentioned in Chapter 6. The focus of this chapter is on the widely circulated notion that Jewish parents and other family members did not want their young women to go into nursing.

Chapter 8 includes a discussion of the experiences of the respondents from the perspective of "as others see us." The discussion focuses primarily on expressions of anti-Semitism from the community at large and on "anti-nurse" sentiments from the Jewish community. Chapter 9 has a description of "as we see ourselves" from the perspective of our Jewish background and how it has influenced our life and career experiences. Chapter 10 includes a description of the networking of Jewish nurses through the nurses councils of Hadassah and indicates the progress of the nurses councils since their establishment in 1990.

Part III—Lest We Forget

This section has one chapter and features nursing in juxtaposition with the military. Wars and the military have markedly influenced the development of nursing. Throughout the ages, women came forth to care for the sick and wounded in wartime, and their names and exploits have figured prominently in the annals of nursing history. Actually, Jewish women have not been included. Chapter 11 shows the presence of Jewish women in this role and provides an overview of Jewish nurses in wartime service throughout the 19th and 20th centuries.

$\mathcal{P}$*art I*

Nursing History Revisited:
A Jewish Perspective

1

Biblical And Talmudic Roots

The Origins of Nursing

ursing as we know it today is barely 150 years old, which makes it a young profession when compared with the older disciplines of medicine, law, and teaching. As such, its own identity and position alongside the other learned professions are still being developed as scholars determine the theoretical knowledge that underlies the traditional goal of providing a humanitarian service to members of the community (Winstead-Fry, 1977). The development of nursing as a profession is clearly identified with the pioneer work of Florence Nightingale. Moreover, it is closely associated with the emerging desire of women in the late 19th and early 20th centuries to move out of the domestic sphere into the public arena. This was the era of the "new woman" who sought independence and fulfillment through the pursuit of a rewarding career.

But nursing, as a universal response to human needs, is as old as humankind, with its roots in the distant past of ancient history. The essence of nursing is caring (Benson & McDevitt, 1980). Nursing began because somebody cared—somebody who had compassion for a fellow human being. The noun, nurse, is derived from Middle English *norse, nurice,* from Old French *norrice, nurice,* from Late Latin *nutricia,* and from Latin *nutricius, nutritius,* 'nourishing' (Webster's Dictionary, 1961). Examining the usage of the word *nurse* illustrates the various connotations that have existed throughout history. From antiquity, society has assigned to women the role of nourishing, nurturing, or tending and feeding infants and young children, and, indeed, early references to *nurse* have this connotation.

In time, the word *nurse* took on the meaning of "one who takes care of, looks after, or advises another" (Compact Edition of the Oxford English Dictionary, 1971, p. 1956, first citation 1425

Common Era [C.E.]). The meaning was extended to include "a person, generally a woman, who attends or waits upon the sick; now esp. one properly trained for this purpose" (Compact Edition of the Oxford English Dictionary, 1971, p. 1956, first citation 1590 C.E.). Current definitions have been expanded to include men or women who possess a variety of qualities and skills and perform many sophisticated functions. Or, as one of the contemporary scholars of nursing history has stated, " . . . it is apparent that the meaning of the word has progressed from a term indicating the basic unlearned human activity of suckling an infant to one of a highly learned sophisticated nature" (Donahue, 1985, pp. 3-4). Clearly, these broadened connotations indicate change and expansion of the nursing role.

Standard works in nursing history have described the impact of religion on the progression of nursing in the pre-Nightingale era and have traditionally asserted that the roots of nursing lie in Christianity. Such works have characterized the early development of nursing as an expression of "Christian love and charity" by women devoted to the church. At the same time, they have acknowledged some contributions of "ancient Hebrews." However, while underscoring the role of women and the influence of religion in the development of nursing, they have generally overlooked the Jewish heritage in contemporary nursing, and they have ignored the presence of Jewish women in the profession (Benson, 1993).

To trace the Jewish heritage in nursing, it is necessary to go back to the dawn of civilization, as do many nurse-historians. In examining nursing history from the perspective of Judaism, we should look at the history of related disciplines such as medicine, pharmacology, and public health. It is also important to examine the role of Jewish women in history. Most standard textbooks of nursing history describe the rites and customs of ancient civilizations wherein lie the seeds of many modern day medical, nursing, and health practices. Almost invariably the "ancient Hebrews" are cited for their contributions to all of the health disciplines, specifically with regard to promoting hygiene and sanitation practices. Evidence exists that both men and women were actively involved in these ancient practices.

Health and Disease in Mosaic Law

Customs and traditions related to health and disease among the Hebrews of the Bible were closely tied to their religious beliefs. God was the source of health and illness (Singer, 1904a). Sickness was regarded as an outcome of God's displeasure, and people sought divine intervention for healing (Jakobovits, 1975). God's commandments were transcribed into the written law and had to be scrupulously observed. The rituals and practices were spelled out in the sacred writings of the *Torah*. Loosely translated as "Law" or "Doctrine," *Torah* has a more specific meaning, one that encompasses the notion of "instruction" especially in the practical conduct of human beings. Law, religion, and morality were inseparable and were translated into prescribed activities in the daily lives of the Jewish people. The rules and regulations affected virtually every aspect of human behavior and provided the framework that sustained Jewish society throughout the ages (Grant, 1984).

The Hebrew Scriptures set forth one of the earliest public health movements on record with precise sanitary measures that:

- mandated cleanliness in all areas of living,
- required supervision in the selection and preparation of all foods,
- devised a system of meat inspection, and
- called for the proper disposal of contaminated articles in cases of communicable disease.

Prescribed actions were based on religious principles, called *Mitzvot*, and were established as religious rituals and customs. For example, hand washing was regarded not merely as an elementary act of hygiene, but primarily as a rite of consecration. Personal cleanliness was held to be the door to spiritual purity. "Cleanliness is next to godliness" as a proverb is in accordance with the rabbinic spirit. Priests began their daily service in the Temple by washing their hands. The act of hand washing is accompanied by a prayer or blessing: "Blessed art thou, O Lord our God, Ruler of the Universe, who has hallowed us by thy commandments, and given us the command concerning the washing of the hands."

Basing their teachings on the laws of Moses, the Talmudic Rabbis (2nd-5th centuries C.E.) in their commentaries and interpretations taught the importance of hand washing as a prescribed act of cleanliness. In Leviticus (Hertz, 1975, Leviticus 11:44), God directs the children of Israel to "sanctify yourselves" (*V'hitkadishtem*). The rabbis translated this general principle of religion into life's everyday practices and used it as the basis for the precept of washing the hands before meals. Rabbi Akiba stated it very strongly, but with hyperbole, when he declared that "according to the Law of my colleagues, people who do not wash their hands are deserving of death" (Cohen, 1975, from Berakhot, 53 B).

Women and the Healing Arts—Midwifery Plus

In the biblical era, God alone was the "physician" of Israel, but the practice of medicine by human physicians was legitimized in the *Torah* (Singer, 1904a). From earliest times, in Scripture and by tradition, physicians occupied an exalted status in the Jewish community and were regarded as "messengers of God." Although we do not know whether women were counted in the ranks of these practitioners, it is certain that women in the biblical period played a role in the healing arts. From ancient times, in addition to fulfilling their functions as nurturers and caregivers in the home and family, Hebrew women were educated for similar public roles as midwives, surgeons, anatomists, and teachers (Hurd-Mead, 1977).

The earliest reference to *nurse* in the Scriptures is found in the Book of Genesis in which Rebekah's nurse (*meineket*) is identified as a woman named Deborah (Hertz, 1975, Genesis 24:59, 35:8). In the second chapter of Exodus, reference to a nurse is made when Miriam says to Pharaoh's daughter, ". . . shall I go and call thee a nurse (*meineket*) of the Hebrew women, that she may nurse the child for thee?" (Hertz, 1975, Exodus 2: 7-9). These citations clearly refer to the role of "nourishing, nurturing, or tending and feeding infants and young children." Other references to a more expanded nursing role appear in Genesis where there is mention of the unnamed midwife (*meyaledet*) who attended Tamar at the birth of her twins (Hertz, 1975, Genesis 38:28).

In the Book of Exodus there is a description of the midwives, Shiphrah and Puah, who refused to obey Pharaoh's command to kill the newborn male children among the Hebrews (Hertz, 1975, Exodus 1:15-21). According to the Scriptures and the commentaries, the midwives were "godfearing" or they "revered God" (*Vatireno hamyaldot et haelohim*). And so they ignored Pharaoh and obeyed the inner voice of human compassion that is the guiding spirit of nursing practice (Benson, 1994). Their show of defiance was perhaps the earliest recorded act of civil disobedience and, interestingly enough, one that was perpetrated by women.

Although there were only seven short biblical verses about Shiphrah and Puah, these two women have been extolled as heroines for their contribution to the people of Israel. We do not know anything about their origin or whether they were Hebrew or Egyptian. Various interpretations in the Talmud suggest that these midwives really were Yocheved and Miriam (the mother and sister of Moses) or Yocheved and Elisheva (the mother and sister-in-law of Moses) (Bash, 1993). According to one rabbinic interpretation, the names Shiphrah and Puah are a play on Hebrew words. Shiphrah's name was said to relate to the Hebrew word *shafar* (to clean), which referred to her task of cleaning the infant right after birth. Puah's name was regarded as a play on the Hebrew word *po'ah* (to sing), which referred to the act of singing sweet songs to the infants so that they would not cry and give away their whereabouts to Pharaoh's spies (Mayer, 1996).

Whoever they were, Shiphrah and Puah emerged as the forerunners and role models for women in the healing arts. In the rabbinic and Talmudic tradition, these two women of the Bible were held in high esteem for their wisdom, expertise, and praiseworthy demeanor. In the *Mishnah*, the collection of teachings that were based on scriptural verses and became known as the "Oral Law," the rabbis discuss the midwife and her responsibilities within the context of observing the Sabbath, but they do not refer to her in the ordinary sense of *meyaledet* or *birth helper* (Albeq, 1959, Rosh Hashanah 2:5 and Shabbat 18:3). They use the term *cha-*

Artist's portrayal of Biblical midwives, Shiphrah and Puah

chamah or "wise woman," from which is derived the English *wise-woman,* the German *die weise Frau,* and the French *la sage-femme,* all of which denote *midwife* (Mayer, 1996). Jewish women continued to play a significant role in the healing arts in the postbiblical era and throughout the Middle Ages. For example, according to one source, in the 12th century C.E., Jews were considered to be the best physicians, and the practice of midwifery as well as of gynecology and obstetrics was left to their women (Hurd-Mead, 1977).

Ancient Judaic Precepts

Apart from the Mosaic principles relating to sanitation and hygiene, the two Judaic precepts that are most closely allied with the concept of nursing and the origin of hospitals are expressed by the terms *Hesed* and *Bikkur Holim. Hesed,* which is regarded as a divine quality, encompasses acts of loving kindness, mercy, and compassion. *Bikkur Holim,* which is held as a sacred duty, is the act or *Mitzvah* of visiting the sick (Friedenwald, 1967). Such acts have always been associated with caring, a quality that has been identified as the essence of nursing practice. Nurse-historians assert that the raison d'etre of nursing was derived from the precept of "visiting the sick," which they have generally claimed as an act of Christian love and charity, but one which we see is rooted in a much older Judaic tradition.

In a similar manner, the establishment of the hospital as an institution is often attributed to Fabiola, a devout Christian dedicated to "good works" in the 4th century C.E. Fabiola is prominent in nursing history as one of the group of Roman matrons who had converted to Christianity in the 4th and 5th centuries C.E. Fabiola and her contemporaries were independent women of the upper class who had acquired great wealth. They devoted themselves to relief work and to caring for the sick, as recorded in the writings of St. Jerome (Donahue, 1985). Interestingly enough, St. Jerome characterized Fabiola's efforts as "transplanting the terebinth of Abraham to Ausonian shores" (Singer, 1904b, p. 479). He was referring to the Hebraic-Judaic philanthropic tradition of extending comfort, hospitality, and kindness to strangers—qualities associated with *Hesed*—as epitomized in the story of Abraham at Mamre (Hertz, 1975, Genesis 18:1-8).

From this perspective, while the origin of the hospital has traditionally been attributed to the early Christians, its earliest conception can be traced to a Hebrew tradition long before the rise of Christianity. Among the Hebrews of the Bible, the hospital, as a designated unit for housing the sick, was probably exemplified in two ways: (a) a home set aside as a refuge for strangers where a portion would be reserved for those who became ill, and (b) a "house of separation" required for cases of "leprosy" (Singer, 1904b). So far as can be determined, the sick and infirm were most likely cared for in their own homes, and the commandment of *Bikkur Holim* or "visiting the sick" was incumbent on all members of the community. Indeed, this Judaic precept has been characterized as "one of the most conspicuous duties which Jews of all times included under the general head of charity" (Abrahams, 1932, p. 467).

Summary

Jewish roots in nursing are revealed through an examination of ancient Judaic texts and the early history of the Jewish people. Clearly many of the identifying features of nursing, which have been attributed to Christianity in standard works on nursing history, can, in fact, be traced back to older and well established rules and customs that are part of the Judaic tradition. The biblical text identifies the role of women not only as nurturers and caregivers in the family and in the community, but also as practitioners of the healing arts. Thus we find several references to the "nurse" in the role of nourishing, nurturing, or tending and feeding infants and young children. We also find references to an expanded nursing role in the practice of the midwife. These are roles that embody the act of human caring and compassion, which has been characterized as the essence of nursing. It was one such singular act on the part of the two biblical midwives, Shiphrah and Puah, which earned them special commendation in the history of the Jewish people. They were recognized not only for their compassionate care, but also for their courageous stand against tyranny and for their dedication to the preservation of life—qualities that are essentially valued in nursing practice.

References

Abrahams, I. (1932). *Jewish life in the middle ages.* New edition enlarged and revised by Cecil Roth. London: Edward Goldston, Ltd.

Albeq, H. (Ed). (1959). *The Mishnah* (in Hebrew). Rosh Hashanah 2:5; Shabbat 18:3. Jerusalem: The Bialik Institute.

Bash, D. M. (1993, Winter). Biblical midwives. *Bulletin of the American Association for the History of Nursing,* 37(7), 7.

Benson, E. R. (1993, March). Public health nursing and the Jewish contribution. *Public Health Nursing,* 10, 55-57.

Benson, E. R. (1994). Jewish nurses: A multicultural perspective. *Journal of the New York State Nurses Association,* 25, 8-10.

Benson, E. R., & McDevitt, J. Q. (1980). *Community health and nursing practice* (2nd ed., p. 35). Englewood Cliffs, NJ: Prentice-Hall.

Cohen, A. (1975). *Everyman's Talmud.* New York: Schocken Books.

Compact edition of the Oxford English dictionary. (1971). New York, NY: The Oxford University Press.

Donahue, M. P. (1985). *Nursing: The finest art.* St. Louis, MO: Mosby.

Friedenwald, H. (1967). *The Jews and medicine: Essays. Vol. II.* New York City, NY: Ktav Publishing House.

Grant, M. (1984). *History of ancient Israel* (p. 147). New York: Scribner's.

Hertz, J. H. (Ed.). (1975). *The Pentateuch and Haftorahs.* Genesis 18:1-8; 24:59; 35:8; 38:28, Exodus 1:15-21; 2:7-9, Leviticus 11:44 (2nd ed.). London: Soncino Press.

Hurd-Mead, K. C. (1977). *A history of women in medicine.* New York, NY: AMS Press.

Jakobovits, I. (1975). *Jewish medical ethics.* New York: Bloch Company.

Mayer, S. L. (1996). *The Jewish experience in nursing in America: 1881 to 1955* (p. 13). (Doctoral Dissertation). Ann Arbor, MI: University Microfilms International.

Singer, I. (Ed.). (1904a). *The Jewish encyclopedia. Vol. VIII* (p. 409). New York, NY: Funk & Wagnalls.

Singer, I. (Ed.) (1904b). *The Jewish encyclopedia. Vol. VI* (p. 479). New York, NY: Funk & Wagnalls.

Webster's third new international dictionary of the English language. (1961). Chicago: Merriam.

Winstead-Fry, P. (1977). The need to differentiate a nursing self. *American Journal of Nursing,* 77, 1452-1454.

2

✡ Nursing and The "Middle Period" Of Jewish History

The "Middle Period" of Jewish history, according to Jewish historians, does not coincide exactly with the Middle Ages in the history of Western civilization, that is, the 5th through 15th centuries C.E. For example, Jacob Marcus designates the Middle Period as the 4th through 18th centuries C.E. Marcus sets the beginning of this period at 315 C.E. with Emperor Constantine's enactment of restrictive laws against the Jews, and he goes up to 1791, with the onset of the process of emancipation in France (Marcus, 1938). *The Encyclopedia Judaica* (Roth & Wigoder, 1971), on the other hand, designates the era that extends from the second-third centuries C.E. to the early 19th century as the Middle Period of Jewish history, beginning approximately with the disintegration of the Jewish state and continuing through the rise of the Enlightenment period. Thus, while authoritative Judaic sources may not necessarily agree on specific dates, they point out that this period starts earlier and ends later in Jewish history than the time designated as the Middle Ages in Western history.

A People Without a Country

After the destruction of their Temple and the loss of their homeland at the end of the 1st century C.E., the Jews were forced into exile. A people without a country, they were scattered over many parts of the world, in what was referred to as the Diaspora, or dispersion. Wherever they were allowed to settle, they tried to become part of the community in which they lived. At the same time they sought ways to uphold the customs and traditions of their distinctive way of life in which they yearned and prayed for their ancient homeland. Devoid of civil power, the Jews sought to dwell in harmony with the dominant population by living up to the ancient Judaic precept enunciated in Jeremiah (29:7) exhorting them to "seek the peace" and "pray for" the "city" where they were allowed to reside in exile.

However, throughout this period in their history, whether they dwelled in European lands under Christendom or in other areas that came under the domination of Islam, the Jewish people were always regarded as outsiders, unbelievers, and foreigners. They often found themselves politically vulnerable and socially excluded in a hostile environment. They were forced to wear special clothing or badges to set them apart from the rest of the population. At the close of the 11th century, they were singled out by the Crusaders as targets for acts of wanton brutality in a manner that presaged the perpetration of the 20th century Holocaust in World War II.

Barred from virtually every occupation and denied admission to local societies and guilds, Jews were obliged to resort to the practice of money-lending as a major means of livelihood. Their well-being and security often depended on the whims of local rulers or the vagaries of higher authorities such as the established Church in Rome. They found that their very existence required delicate balancing and great skill in the politics of accommodation. Despite all these barriers, they often achieved prosperity and a relatively decent standard of living (Baskin, 1991).

While they were subject to the rules and statutes of the principalities in which they lived, the Jewish people also had their own form of self-government with a communal structure and a set of laws by which their daily lives were regulated. It has been said that in the period between the 6th and 11th centuries C.E., the "Talmud became entrenched as a comprehensive guide of Jewish conduct in everyday life" (Zolty, 1993, p. 133). Within strict limits established by the state authorities, the Jewish community was granted autonomy to administer Jewish law through their rabbinical courts and to settle legal disputes among their own people.

Women in the Middle Period

Long before the official creation of ghettos in the towns and cities of Italy, Spain, and other parts of Europe, Jews voluntarily congregated in separate areas where they established their own communal organizations and services (Abrahams, 1958). Every sphere of their daily lives was governed by the rules and precepts of *halakha* (defined as the body of Jewish law supplementing scriptural law and forming especially the legal aspects of the Talmud). So far as we can tell, *halakhic* law was also a major factor in determining the position of Jewish women throughout the Middle Period.

It is only in recent decades that the role and status of women in medieval Europe—non-Jewish as well as Jewish—has emerged as a topic worthy of academic study. Scholarship in this area has advanced primarily through Women's Studies and Jewish Women's Studies. To be sure, work on this topic has been hampered by the dearth of historical sources on events of the early Middle Ages and the lack of data about the part played by women (Amt, 1993; Labarge, 1986; Shahar, 1983). Scholarly sources of information point out that the role of medieval women was largely determined by their social class; hence, these sources suggest, the role of women should be examined in relation to their place in the established social order (Labarge, 1986).

However, medieval Europe was an essentially male-oriented society that categorized women of all classes as inferior human beings. The general belief was that men had a God-given right of dominance over their wives, whose main purpose in life was to bear their children. Women had no identity apart from their husbands, and their lives were bound up in home and family responsibilities. The most notable exception to this rule was found among those Christian women who joined orders where their lives were essentially dedicated to prayer and religious service. Many of these sisterhoods were established specifically to provide nursing care for the sick and are often cited by nurse-historians as early prototypes for the development of nursing.

Religious orders of women do not exist in Judaism. The notion of a Jewish woman vowing to dedicate herself to the service of God was obviated by the reality that her "proper place" was in the home and with the family. The man, on the other hand, occupied the intellectual sphere of learning, study, and scholarly debate (Lacks, 1980). The woman's first duty was to serve her husband and facilitate his fulfilling the commandment to study the *Torah*. The Jewish woman, like her Christian counterpart, did not have the same legal, communal, and social status as did the man (Lacks, 1980). The "noblest calling" of a Jewish woman—her *b'rakha* or blessing—was to bear her husband's children. Through motherhood she achieved "equality" with man.

Throughout the Middle Period of Jewish history, women's lives were not part of the Jewish intellectual experience, but were considered central to Jewish survival. While men were responsible for the "official tradition," women were the bearers of tradition in the private sphere, an especially crucial role in times of rapid change and political turmoil (Lacks, 1980). A significant part of a woman's responsibility to preserve tradition was dictated by the laws and customs of *tzniut* (the laws and customs of modesty). Strictly speaking, the precept governing modesty refers to privacy (Zolty, 1993). Modesty is propriety in words and deeds and has been broadly characterized as a "prerequisite for true religious observance for Jews of both sexes" (Aiken 1992, p. 130). In its application, however, *tzniut*'s proscriptions and prohibitions have been heavily weighted against women and have had a restricting effect on their activities, especially in the public arena (Plaskow, 1990).

Against this backdrop describing Jewish women in the Middle Period, Judith Baskin (1991) makes some striking observations. "Jewish women," she says, "were active participants in the family economy" (p. 102). According to one source "[Jewish women] went out to conduct negotiations with feudal princes and with other Jewish and gentile merchants" (p. 104). Baskin notes further that, despite the *halakhic* rules of modesty, many Jewish women in the Middle Ages, in fact, experienced autonomy, independence, and productive activity in the outside world, as follows:

> During their husbands' absences on business, women ran the family's affairs. . . . Women engaged in all kinds of commercial operations and occupations. . . . Widows would frequently continue their financial activities, occasionally in partnership with another woman. Such undertakings, which could be extremely complex, undoubtedly required literacy and training in mathematics and bookkeeping skills. Some women were probably involved in craft activities, as well, and there are also some references in Christian sources to independent Jewish women who practiced medicine (p. 104).

Jews and the Healing Arts in the Middle Period

Jewish men and women played a significant role in medicine during the Middle Ages as practitioners and scholars, and they were renowned for their knowledge, skill, and devotion. Jews were involved in establishing the first medical school at Salerno, which achieved its greatest fame in the 10th and 11th centuries, and Jewish women studied there (Hurd-Mead, 1977). The Church was never comfortable with the enviable reputation acquired by Jewish physicians and tried at various times to suppress their activities (Abrahams, 1958). However, Church regulations in the 13th century banning Jews from practicing medicine were largely ignored because Jewish physicians excelled in this field. In fact, it has been noted that, despite the ban, they were frequently retained as chief doctors to the royal families of Europe (Hurd-Mead, 1977). However, as the influence of the Church in these matters spread, Jewish physicians had to resort to practicing in secret.

A Jewish tradition of medical ethics and practice had been developed very early. Although the Talmud was not a book of medicine, it contained detailed information on numerous medical matters (Keller, 1966). *Chochmat ha-refua* or the art of healing was identified with the Jewish tradition of caring. The Jewish approach to healing incorporated the unity of body and soul. Judaism placed great value on maintaining a healthy body (Abrahams, 1958). Hygiene was of utmost importance, and observance of divine laws was regarded as the greatest measure of disease prevention. Because of the close relationship between medicine and religion, it was not uncommon to find rabbis who practiced medicine. Perhaps the most notable example was the sage Maimonides (Rabbi Moses ben Maimon or "Rambam" 1135-1204), whose 12th century writings are still regarded as classic works.

Among the Jewish health care practitioners of the Middle Ages, Jewish women were in great demand. They were appreciated for their benevolence and devotion. Wherever they practiced, they exalted the women of the Bible as their prototypes. As mentioned earlier in Chapter 1, midwifery and obstetrics and gynecology were their special areas of practice. They were also known as skilled surgeons and oculists, and they achieved recognition not only as practitioners but also as writers and translators of medical texts. Despite the difficulties imposed by the Church, several Jewish women distinguished themselves in medicine between the 12th and 15th centuries in cities such as Paris, Florence, and Frankfurt. For example, Antonia Daniello was honored by the medical school at Florence where she held a prominent position from 1386 to 1408; in Frankfurt, the archives between 1389 and 1497 list 15 Jewish women who practiced various medical specialties; records from 15th century Passau show that a Jewish woman, Jacopa of Passau, "succored its plague victims with tender care" (Hurd-Mead, 1977, p. 276, 312).

The "Hospital" in the Jewish Community

The closest equivalent to a hospital described in Talmudic literature was a type of hospice or inn designated by the community to provide food and shelter to needy travelers or to the homeless. It is assumed that such establishments were also used for travelers who became ill while passing through an area, although there is no specific mention of this practice in existing sources (Marcus, 1947). In the early synagogues, it was customary to set aside a part of the building as a shelter for itinerant Jews (Landman, 1941). This type of hospice or refuge was referred to as a *hekdesh*, a term that along with *bet hekdesh haaniim* was first used for "hospital" in 11th century Cologne (Singer, 1904). The term *hekdesh* is of ancient origin, going back to the Essenes, and it refers to their voluntarily handing over their land and property to the poor (Friedenwald, 1967). (The Essenes were members of an ancient Jewish sect of ascetics and mystics from the 2nd century B.C.E. to the 2nd century C.E.)

In the 13th, 14th, and 15th centuries, the existence of the *hekdesh* as a hospital, but more likely as a refuge, was recorded in several cities of Central Europe (now Germany) (Singer, 1904). The transformation of the *hekdesh* to the hospital was gradual. Reference was made to a small "hospital" in Berlin by the middle of the 16th century and to "hospitals" in Rome in the 17th century. It was in the 18th century that Jewish hospitals, especially intended for the care and treatment of the sick, were established— the *Beth Holim* of London in 1747 and the *Krankenhaus* of Berlin in 1753 (Singer, 1904).

With respect to the organization and staffing of hospitals during the Middle Ages, the situation in the Jewish community was different from that of the community at large. Throughout the Christian world of that era, hospitals were established and run by religious orders of men and women as well as by the Knights Hospitallers of the Crusades. The situation was different also with regard to "nursing care," which, in the Christian world, was largely performed by religious orders of nuns and monks. And, as we have already noted, there were no religious orders of women in the Jewish world.

Care of the Sick

During the Middle Period of Jewish history, it was through the communal response to the religious commandment of *bikkur holim* and to the precept of *hesed* (see Chapter 1) that nursing care was provided in Jewish communities. The acts of loving kindness and visiting the sick were counted among "the most meritorious acts of true charity" (Jacobovits, 1975, p. 106). As we have noted, these were very old customs under the general heading of charity in the Jewish tradition, and they were incumbent on all members of the community. Harriet Naiman (1970) identifies a general philosophy of nursing in the teachings of the 13th century sage, Nachmanides, who laid out a plan for visiting the sick, which was organized into three parts as follows:

> First, all members of the community are required to visit the ill because a sick person gains greatly from the social comfort of friends. Second, it is incumbent on the visitors to see to the needs of the patient. It is one's duty not only to seek out the needs, but to see that they are fulfilled as well. Then, and not till then, can the third part of the commandment—prayers for the health of the patient—be offered (pp. 2378-2379).

With the information that is available about the existence of Jewish hospitals in the Middle Ages, it is assumed that the sick were basically cared for in their own homes and visited by their coreligionists (their fellow Jews) who, at times, probably filled a "nursing role" by providing hands-on care (Landman, 1941). In general, it is believed that these visitors were men, but, according to one source (Baskin, 1991), apparently it was not uncommon for Jewish women also to go out into the community to fulfill the commandment of *bikkur holim* (visiting the sick). Baskin writes about a man who extols his wife's wisdom and virtues while grieving over her murder at the hands of the Crusaders: "Wise in speech was she . . . buying milk for those who studied and hiring teachers by means of her toil . . . she ran to visit the sick . . ." (p. 106). According to another source, "women were notoriously tender to the sick . . . Jewish men were nursed by women, but the women were not nursed by men" (Abrahams, 1958, p. 330). A reference is also made in the writings of Jacob Marcus (1947) who notes that as far back as the medieval Jewish hospices, women were taken in and cared for by female attendants (p. 139).

A notable development was the creation of benevolent societies, the so-called *hevra kadisha*, in response to the widespread devastation brought on by the epidemics that were prevalent in Europe in the Middle Ages (Abrahams, 1958). Existing methods of providing care had broken down under the strain, and new measures were required. The *hevra kadisha* (holy league or holy brotherhood) could be traced back to the 4th century C.E. when its original purpose was to arrange for proper burial of the dead. In later times, this type of organization provided care for the sick and dying, supplied medicines, distributed warm clothing, and performed other charitable acts of loving kindness (Abrahams, 1958). Marcus refers to the *hevra kadisha* organizations that existed in Jewish communities in Germany in the 16th, 17th, and 18th centuries. Staffed primarily by men, they performed services for the dying and provided "nursing care" in the home. They also assumed responsibility for providing care in some of the local Jewish "hospitals" that had been established (Marcus, 1947). The role of women in these men's organizations was limited to caring for other women as the need arose.

Marcus (1947) also points out that in a typical late medieval Jewish community, medical services would include not only physicians, surgeons, and midwives but also male and female hospital-attendants, sick-attendants for the poor in their homes, paid supervisors of sick-care, and special attendants for contagious diseases and for periods of emergency. By the 17th century, records show that Jewish women were involved in "nursing" in their communities. For example, hospital nurses and midwives were listed among the 60 occupations tabulated for the Jews of Prague in the 17th century (Marcus, 1947). Also in the 17th century there were loosely organized societies of "Pious Women" (*nashim zadkani-yyot*) serving the Jews living in German principalities (Marcus, 1947). In the 18th century, "sick-care societies," which were devoted specifically to the care of the sick, had been established by Jewish women in several German cities, and the existing *hevra kadisha* societies were employing nurses and female caregivers (Marcus, 1947).

Summary

During the long stretch of time designated as the Middle Period of Jewish history, we find that Jews in Europe led a very precarious existence. However, despite inhospitable conditions in the surrounding world, they survived and, at times, even prospered in their own communities under a form of self-government based on their ancient laws and traditions. Men were accorded official status and recognition in this society, and, although numerous restrictions were imposed by custom, women held a dominant position in various circumscribed aspects of life.

We also note that Jewish women were active in their own communities as caregivers in a role that nurse-historians typically identify in describing "nursing" in the pre-Nightingale era. To be sure, Judaism never had religious orders of women, such as those in the Christian world that were responsible for establishing this early tradition in nursing. Nonetheless, the participation of Jewish women in the "art of nursing practice" during that era was not unlike that of their Christian counterparts. Jewish women were, in fact, very much involved in the community's program of providing care and comfort for the sick.

References

Abrahams, I. (1958). *Jewish life in the middle ages.* New York: Meridian Books, The World Publishing Co.

Aiken, L. (1992). *To be a Jewish woman.* Northvale, NJ: Jason Aronson.

Amt, E. (1993). *Women's lives in medieval Europe: A sourcebook.* New York: Routledge.

Baskin, J. (1991). Jewish women in the middle ages. In Judith R. Baskin (Ed.), *Jewish women in historical perspective.* Detroit: Wayne State University Press.

Friedenwald, H. (1967). *The Jews and medicine. Vol. II.* New York, NY: KTAV Publishing.

Hurd-Mead, K. C. (1977). *A history of women in medicine.* Haddam, CT: The Haddam Press.

Jacobovits, I. (1975). *Jewish medical ethics.* New York: Bloch Publishing.

Keller, W. (1966). *Diaspora.* New York: Harcourt, Brace and World.

Labarge, M.W. (1986). *Women in medieval life: A small sound of the trumpet.* London: Hamish Hamilton.

Lacks, R. (1980). *Women and Judaism: Myth, history and struggle.* Garden City, NY: Doubleday.

Landman, I. (Ed.). (1941). *The universal Jewish encyclopedia. Vol. 5.* New York: Funk and Wagnalls.

Marcus, J. R. (1938). *The Jew in the medieval world: A source book.* Cincinnati: The Sinai Press.

Marcus, J. R. (1947). *Communal sick-care in the German ghetto.* Cincinnati: The Hebrew Union College Press.

Naiman, H. (1970). Nursing in Jewish law. *American Journal of Nursing, 70*(11), 2378-2379.

Plaskow, J. (1990). *Standing again at Sinai.* San Francisco: Harper.

Roth, C., & Wigoder, G. (Eds.). (1971). *Encyclopedia Judaica. Vol. 11.* Jerusalem: Keter Publishing.

Shahar, S. (1983). *The fourth estate: A history of women in the middle ages.* New York: Methuen.

Singer, I. (Ed.). (1904). *The Jewish Encyclopedia. Vol. VI.* New York: Funk and Wagnalls.

Zolty, S. P. (1993). *"And all your children shall be learned": Women and the study of Torah in Jewish law and history.* Northvale, NJ: Jason Aronson.

3

 **The Dawning of a New Era
and the Nightingale Legacy**

*A*n exploration of the Jewish heritage in nursing reveals that the 19th century was a most significant period. The end of the 18th century had signaled the dawning of a new era that set the stage for:
- transformation in the lives of Jews,
- change in the status of women, and
- progress in the development of nursing as a profession.

Jewish Life in Eastern Europe

During the late 18th and early 19th centuries, many Jewish people dwelled throughout Eastern Europe, with their heaviest concentration inside the Russian Empire's "Pale of Settlement." The Pale was a large geographic area designated by the government in the 1790s as the only place where Jews were permitted to reside—except for a privileged few who, because of some unusual talent, were allowed to live in cities. In tracing the chain of events that led to this situation, we go back to the period following the excesses of the Crusades. At that point in their history, many Jews, predominantly from German principalities, fled for their lives and went to Poland, where they found refuge. They took with them their customs, religion, and Judeo-Germanic language, which developed into Yiddish and became the language of the Jews of Eastern Europe (Dubnow, 1975).

In Poland, the Jews were allowed to settle and to carry on trade. From the outset, they were ghettoized, typically inside a little town or *shtetl* where they could create their own self-governing body, or *Kahal*. The *Kahal* dominated the everyday lives of Jewish people, and it was also responsible for collecting the taxes that the ruling princes demanded from the Jewish community. The *Kahal* had the authority to organize its own communal infrastructure through which community services were provided and community activities were carried out. Special emphasis was placed on education. Educational institutions, which could be found even in the smallest and poorest communities, were intended for boys only, and studies were concentrated essentially on religious topics. Poland, in the 16th century, had been a recognized center of Jewish learning, and for the Jewish people of Europe it became the "legitimate seat of its national hegemony" (Dubnow, 1975, p. 139).

For many years, under the *Kahal* structure, the Jews managed to live in Poland in a state of relative "security." However, their very existence was seriously threatened when a series of economic and national developments within the larger community led to a wave of persecution, pogroms (i.e., officially organized attacks targeting Jews), and massacres. These acts of violence erupted in the 17th and 18th centuries and were an ominous forerunner of greater tragedies that lay ahead. In 1795, after the third partition of Poland (the first partition occurred in 1772 and the second in 1793), the territories occupied by the greatest number of Jews were taken over by the Russian Empire, and the Jews were confined to the Pale of Settlement. The brutal Czarist government, in establishing the Pale for Jews, restricted their place of residence, limited their freedom of movement, imposed heavy taxes, and, in general, perpetuated and intensified their misery, poverty, and degradation.

These wretched conditions in the daily lives of Jews in 19th century Russia, compounded by periodic outbreaks of officially orchestrated violence against them, fueled their yearning for freedom from oppression. In varying degrees they began to respond to the waves of change that had drifted in from Western Europe, where people were experiencing the liberating effects of the Protestant Reformation, the Enlightenment, and the French Revolution. By 1870, most countries of Central and Western Europe had granted some measure of equal rights to Jews. Of course, only a minority of world Jewry was thus enfranchised, leaving the overwhelming majority of Jews, who were still in Russia, in virtual bondage to their rulers.

As the 19th century progressed, the Jews in Russia began to seek political liberation from the Czar's oppression and personal liberation from the stultifying confines of ghetto life. In their struggle for liberation, some formed their own organizations and entered into revolutionary movements with or without non-Jewish "comrades." Others sought "national" Jewish liberation by joining forces with the Zionist movement (i.e., the movement to establish a Jewish national state). Still others sought liberation through "enlightenment" and were attracted to the *Haskalah* movement. And many sought the ultimate in liberation by thronging to the ports of embarkation for massive emigration to the West, chiefly to America, the "Golden Land" (Roth, 1970).

Nineteenth Century Women in Europe

Throughout the 19th century, rumblings for liberation were felt from other quarters. For example, women everywhere were raising their voices in a struggle for emancipation. During that era, often referred to in Western culture as the Victorian Age, women were still a subordinate group in a society that was universally male-dominated. Nineteenth century women have been the subject of renewed interest to contemporary historians and social critics who seek to identify and interpret the place of women in history. New insights have been contributed, for example, to issues such as whether women of the Victorian era wielded power and influence on society, and, if so, to what extent. There are unanswered questions and differences of interpretation with regard to these issues.

Most historians agree, however, that a woman's place in 19th century Victorian society was severely restricted. Sex roles were solidified to an extreme. Women were subordinate to men and were relegated to domestic activities; at the same time they were designated the guardians of morality as "loving wives" and "angelmothers." Many faced an impossible choice as a result of the Industrial Revolution, which had affected every level of 19th century society and was especially detrimental to women. Industrialization moved people into factories and put an end to home industries forcing women to choose between staying home with their children or going out to earn wages, however meager (Benson, 1990).

In addition, the 19th century witnessed an increased number of democratic institutions from which women were excluded. Women of all social classes responded to the ideal of egalitarianism, but they were not part of the political process, and they could not vote. Before the century was over, women were organizing to work for voting rights and to correct the inequities under which they labored. Their suffrage campaign lasted many years and did not bear results until well into the 20th century.

Women in 19th century Western Europe and America were experiencing varying degrees of success in their quest for education and for greater participation in public activities. Some Jewish women along with their non-Jewish counterparts achieved recognition as poets, writers, intellectual leaders, organizers of cultural salons, and patronesses of worthy public projects (Henry & Taitz, 1978). The opportunities that were opening to Western women, however marginal, were slower in reaching women in Eastern Europe. The totalitarian regime of the autocratic czars was not conducive to advancing the cause of women's rights. Numerous intellectually gifted and highly educated women from the privileged classes in Russia were active in humanitarian causes or campaigns for social justice (Lindenmeyr, 1993). However, most women in 19th century Russia, including Jewish women, lived under conditions of extreme cultural, social, and economic deprivation.

Jewish Women in Eastern Europe

The Jewish women of *shtetl* life in czarist Russia were the forebears of thousands of contemporary Jewish women in America. *Shtetl* life revolved around the home and the synagogue. Synagogue life belonged to the men and boys, and Jewish learning was reserved for them. Jewish women were relegated to the home, the garden, and the marketplace. Attending to the household was a never-ending responsibility. Jewish women were taught by their mothers to conduct a "proper home," be self-sufficient, and sacrifice for male family members. It was said that "women earned and men learned" (Mayer, 1996, p. 38). Women were taught a trade and expected to earn their living through self-employment or through employment by members of the family; working for others was shunned. Even though *shtetl* women earned a living, they gained little status or financial reward.

The marketplace was special in that it afforded women of the *shtetl* the opportunity to develop business acumen and to learn a language other than Yiddish (i.e., Russian or Polish). Most of these women had no formal education. However, a lucky few were taught how to read or, at least, how to write their names. Some girls studied on their own, begged their brothers to teach them, or—occasionally—were tutored. The women who could read were important to the other religiously observant *shtetl* women. They would help lead those women in prayer in their segregated section of the synagogue. They could also read from the *Tsene-*

rene, the Yiddish-language version of the Pentateuch that was specially designed for them.

Jewish women (and men) in the *shtetl* lived at poverty level in primitive housing. Burlap sacks filled with straw and hay were tucked into the walls as insulation. The roofs were thatched, the floors were earthen, and no indoor plumbing was present. Existence in these wretched surroundings was under constant threat of disruption or extinction by officially organized capricious and wanton acts of oppression and brutality emanating from the Russian government and the Orthodox Church. The infamous May laws of 1882 prohibited Jews from owning or renting land, expelled them from towns where they had lived for generations, and imposed quotas that restricted the numbers of any settlers allowed. All the while, the pogroms continued. Not surprisingly, between 1881 and 1914, approximately one-third of all Jews left Eastern Europe.

Jewish Women Immigrants in America

The Eastern European Jewish immigrants who came to America welcomed opportunities for equal participation and acceptance in an open society. The idea of equal opportunity captivated the psyche of most immigrant Jews. Among all of the immigrant population groups, it was the young Jewish women who were most eager to become Americanized. Many of them went right to work in the garment industry, and quite a few became activists in the trade union movement (Benson & Selekman, 1992). Immigrant Jewish women found in America a climate that they could not have imagined in their wildest dreams back in the *shtetl*. They had their first taste of personal freedom, which allowed them to seek independence and fulfillment through the pursuit of a rewarding career in the public sphere. During this period, when nursing was coming into its own, the Jewish press was asking why more Jewish women did not choose this profession, which was portrayed in a very positive light (Michael Reese Hospital, 1895; The Trained Nurse, 1898; Important Exhibitions, 1898).

Articles appearing in Jewish publications encouraged young immigrant women to go into nursing, and they promoted it as a worthy occupation for young Jewish women of that era. In a description of Jewish "working-girls," Mary M. Cohen (Glanz, 1976) extolled the option of a nursing career as follows:

Surely, among a number of kind-hearted, unselfish girls, some are fitted by nature to adopt the profession of a nurse! What more worthy vocation for a young woman after she has gone through the two year's course in the Training School, acquired the science of nursing, disciplined her mind and steadied her nerves, than to move henceforward as a skillful, tender guardian among the ill and weary of her people! The salary of a capable, trustworthy nurse is very large and well repays the time expended in preparation for the work; but that is not all. The nurse may have spiritual duties and privileges to perform; she is more frequently with the patient than the doctor is; she sees the fatigue, the depression, perhaps the agony of the sufferer; and it may often be her office to brighten, refresh, or soothe the invalid in many ingenious ways. Is there not more soul in this, a greater opportunity for real usefulness than in burning out eyes over the making of fringe! Truly, the labor would be worth while, were the pecuniary rewards small; as it is, a fine and lucrative career stands open to any girl who has even a moderate capacity for taking care of the sick (Cohen, 1883, p. 4).

An article in *The American Jewess*, encouraging young Jewish women to go into nursing, highlighted the accomplishments of Johanne Moritzen, a Jewish woman who came to the United States from Denmark and studied nursing at a hospital in Philadelphia. When she completed her course, she sought additional experience at a hospital in Washington (identified as the Emergency hospital). She then worked for the summer seasons of 1894 and 1895 at the Seaside House in Atlantic City, which was operated under the auspices of the Jewish Maternity Association of Philadelphia. Afterwards, Moritzen accepted a position at the Emergency hospital in Washington. In describing Moritzen's experiences, the article waxed eloquent about the field of nursing:

In an age like the present, rife with arguments and controversies as to what shall be woman's defined sphere and limitations as a wage-earner, it is like balm in Gilead to know that her supremacy receives due homage and acknowledgment in at least one domain, that of professional nursing of the sick. Aside from individual preferences for more masculine vocations, none others offer to the independent-seeking spirit such boundless opportunities for the exercise of natural endowments and temperament. It is the most womanly of all womanly occupations. But while woman possesses as a birthright the fundamental requirements for this noble calling, to succeed as a trained nurse she must have, or require, abundant culture and education. Fresh from the refining influence of home, with a liberal endowment of feminine accomplishments and a sound mental and physical equipment, the candidate for professional honors may safely look beyond the term of probation and subsequent course of training at the hospital (Where Woman Reigns Supreme, 1895, pp. 164-166).

Miss Johanne Moritzen

Source: "Where Woman Reigns Supreme", *The American Jewess* 2(3):164, 1895, December. Courtesy of the Center for Advanced Judaic Studies, University of Pennsylvania.

The Evolution of Nursing: The Jewish Presence

The evolution of nursing in the 19th century is often viewed in terms of the:

1. prevailing gender roles in society,
2. frequent wars and epidemics
3. desire of women to move into the public arena

Throughout the 19th century, women had begun to venture out of the traditional confines of the home in search of fulfillment in their lives by devoting themselves to humanitarian work in the community. In the nursing literature, numerous references are made to 19th century Christian women in religious orders and laywomen in community organizations who volunteered to offer many kinds of help to their fellow human beings in ordinary times. It was in times of crisis, such as the devastating wars and epidemics of the 19th century, that the need for nursing care was dramatically demonstrated. In such periods of crisis, appeals for help would usually be couched in patriotic terms, and nursing became a socially acceptable area of volunteer work for women.

Socially prominent women, often without formal training, played active roles as volunteer "nurses" or used their personal resources to establish organizations of women who would nurse the victims of wars and epidemics. These are the women who are traditionally cited as prototypes in the early development of nursing. Nurse-historians point to this era as a precursor to modern nursing. It was an era in which many American and European women were involved in "good works" of Christian charity that earned them a place in the annals of nursing history. It is fitting to note that, in fact, many dedicated Jewish women were similarly engaged and also merit such recognition (Benson & Selekman, 1992).

In early 19th century America, we find Jewish women who served their communities in accordance with the Judaic commandment of visiting the sick. In 1819, several Jewish "ladies of benevolent instincts" (Wolf & Whiteman, 1975, p. 276) established the Female Hebrew Benevolent Society in Philadelphia. Under the guidance of Rebecca Gratz, a prominent member of the Philadelphia Jewish community, the women of the society established a general welfare program that included a visiting nurse service. Gratz was a highly respected, influential woman in Philadelphia, and she took the initiative in spearheading other welfare and educational projects in the city (Wolf & Whiteman, 1975).

Female benevolent societies had been developed in other Amer-

artist: Thomas Sully

Rebecca Gratz

ican Jewish communities by the 1840s, and these groups of women not only offered nursing care to the sick and dying, but also provided assistance to the needy. A Jewish woman, Penina Moise, who was born in 1797 in Charleston, S.C., set up a system of nursing, without regard to religion or social position, for the victims of the yellow fever epidemic that raged through Charleston in 1854. An unnamed Jewish woman was acclaimed for nursing the townspeople of Natchez, Miss., through yellow fever epidemics, and for this she was greatly loved and highly respected. Rosa Newmark, the wife of Los Angeles' first rabbi, arrived in that city in 1854 and established the Ladies Hebrew Benevolent Society, which provided volunteer nurses for the community (Benson & Selekman, 1992).

It has been noted that nursing in America "had its roots in women's involvement in the Civil War" (Parsons, 1983, pp. 25-29) just as the development of "modern nursing" in England had its roots in the Crimean War. During the Civil War, women in America answered the call for assistance and relief, and Jewish women in the North and South were among those who responded. Their patriotism was genuine despite the fact that throughout the war overt anti-Jewish sentiment existed on both sides of the conflict. Interestingly, some 10,000 Jews fought in the military—about 7,000 for the North and 3,000 for the South.

In the North, the U.S. Sanitary Commission, which coordinated the organization of relief activities, counted among its membership many Jewish citizens. Jewish women's societies, which already existed in major cities, collected funds, prepared bandages and lint, and participated in the Sanitary Commission activities to provide help for the troops. As the needs grew, new groups of Jewish women were formed for the relief of sick and wounded soldiers. The Jews' Hospital in New York, which later became Mount Sinai Hospital, turned a portion of its facilities over to the U.S. government for care of the troops.

The Jews' Hospital in New York

(the original name of the Mount Sinai Hospital).
Source: The Mount Sinai Archives.

In the South, the work of Jewish women in the role of nursing has been documented in their own writings and in the writings of others (Benson & Selekman, 1992). Isabel Adeline Moses was described as the youngest volunteer nurse, who—at the age of 14—worked long hours taking care of the wounded in a Columbus, Ga., hospital. Rosanna (Rosana) Osterman, of Galveston, Texas, a well-to-do, philanthropic member of the Jewish community, turned her home into a hospital for the wounded, where she cared for both Union and Confederate fighting forces; even before the Civil War, Osterman had set up a tent outside her home to nurse victims of the 1853 yellow fever epidemic. Dora Amelia (Levine) Levin tended wounded Confederate soldiers who were brought to a warehouse south of Richmond overlooking the James River (Levin, 1972). Phoebe Yates Levy Pember, who was born in 1823 to a prosperous and cultured Jewish family in Charleston, S.C., served the Confederacy as the Matron of the Chimborazo Hospital in Richmond. A new center for nursing history was opened a few years ago in Virginia, and Pember has been given a place of honor there (Benson & Selekman, 1992).

America in the 1860s witnessed a movement for the creation of Jewish hospitals under the leadership of the eminent Rabbi Isaac Leeser. Rabbi Leeser had identified a need for hospital facilities that could accommodate patients who were religiously observant Jews. By the end of the 1860s several Jewish hospitals were in operation, and as time went on they opened schools of nursing.

In Europe as well as in America many Jewish women could be cited in the annals of nursing history for their prototypical nursing roles throughout the 19th century. A little-known figure, who became a legend in her own time, emerged from the wretched ghettos of mid-19th century czarist Russia. Chana Rochel Werbermacher (1815-1892) came from a very simple background, and although she had no formal training, she was gifted with remarkable insights into human behavior and with an unusual aptitude for scholarship. Modest and unassuming, she became a religious leader, a *rebbe*, in defiance of the traditional bans against women. She risked excommunication by the religious establishment when she assumed the role of a religious leader, successfully practicing the healing arts and wisely counseling the poor and oppressed inhabitants of her community (Winkler, 1991).

Phoebe Yates Levy Pember

Civil War Period 1861-1865
Courtesy of Robert Marcus

Jewish women in Western Europe could also be counted among those who used their personal wealth and other resources to provide care for the sick and needy in times of wars and epidemics. Rahel (Levin) Varnhagen von Ense (1771-1833) was reputed to be one of the leading intellectual and cultural figures of late 18th and early 19th

Rahel Varnhagen, 1817

Portrait from the collections of Uppsala University Library, Uppsala, Sweden
Courtesy of Uppsala University Library

century Berlin's brilliant and elegant salon society. She had expressed a longing for "some profession" in much the same way as Florence Nightingale did at a later date. In the early 1800s, during the Napoleonic wars, Varnhagen was in Prague, where she set up hospital facilities and provided direct care for wounded soldiers. She had the reputation of being a good organizer. Like Nightingale, Rahel Varnhagen felt a sense of personal fulfillment in her nursing role, and during the 1830 cholera epidemic in Berlin, she again volunteered as a nurse. Throughout much of her life, Varnhagen was estranged from the Jewish community. She lived through a stormy, unhappy childhood and rebelled against the rule of a strict, authoritarian father. On the other hand, Varnhagen was devoted to her mother and nursed her through illness (Fink, 1978). An early 20th century feminist author considered her to be the greatest Jewish woman who ever lived (Key, 1913). In fact, Varnhagen had converted to Christianity but in the end expressed regret for having denied her Jewish heritage.

The contribution of Lina Morgenstern in Germany is also noteworthy. "Soup-kitchen Lina," as she was called, worked in the community at large, and in the war of 1866, she set up a soup kitchen to feed the war victims. In the war of 1871, she nursed wounded soldiers. Despite all her humanitarian acts, which extended to non-Jewish as well as Jewish victims, she did not escape vituperative anti-Semitic barbs (Kaplan, 1991).

Jewish women in 19th century Germany served as Red Cross volunteers. They also organized and directed their own societies, which provided nursing care to the sick in their communities. Their services were organized in much the same way as those of the orders of Roman Catholic nuns and Lutheran deaconesses. Members of religious orders in Germany were renowned for their system of nursing even before the initiation of reforms for secular nursing by Florence Nightingale. In fact, it was the model establishment of the Protestant Deaconesses at Kaiserswerth that attracted Florence Nightingale, who spent 3 months there for the only formal training in nursing that she ever received. Toward the end of the century, as Germany progressed in its development of nursing, the first Jewish organizations for training nurses were established in Hamburg in 1892 according to Sokoloff (1992) and in Frankfurt in 1893 according to Benson (1995). Up to that point Jewish women could not hope to train as nurses in Germany because they were required to present baptismal certificates for

Florence Nightingale

Source: Australian Town and Country Journal, 1875

admission to other training programs, including even those that were considered secular.

Modern, Secular Nursing: The Nightingale Legacy

Modern, secular nursing emerged in late 19th century England and became the early model for the establishment of nursing throughout the world. The impetus to the development of professional nursing was provided by the indomitable will and dedicated efforts of Florence Nightingale, who began her work at a time when nursing in England had reached its lowest point. The tradition of nursing service characteristic of the early religious orders had been weakened with the decline of the Church's power and influence in the wake of the Reformation. Municipal hospitals, which had replaced those founded by religious groups, paid scant wages and recruited thieves, slatterns, drunks, and others unfit for the responsibility of providing nursing care. This class of worker was the object of biting satire in Charles Dickens' novel, *Martin Chuzzlewit*, through the characters of *Sairey Gamp* and *Betsey Prig*. Victorian England was ready for fundamental changes in nursing in a period that was marked by other reform movements, and Florence Nightingale emerged as one of the great, dynamic social reformers of that era (Benson & McDevitt, 1980).

Florence Nightingale (1820-1910) was born into a wealthy, socially prominent family, and from both maternal and paternal relatives she was exposed to progressive views and humanitarian ideals. Her maternal grandfather served in Parliament for 46 years, where he was a "champion of abolition, factory workers, dissenters, and Jews" (Hebert, 1981, p. 66). Her paternal grandfather also expressed views that were sympathetic to the rights of Jews in an era that was openly anti-Semitic (Cook, 1942). Nightingale, herself, although of a deeply religious nature and a devout Christian, was very critical of the organized Church and did not tolerate religious discrimination. In 1853, in her first independent position in nursing as Superintendent of the Harley Street Nursing Home, she rejected her Board of Governors' regulation that included Church of England affiliation as a requirement for admission. She insisted on having the authority to admit Roman Catholic and Jewish patients as well (Florence Nightingale at Harley Street, 1970).

From earliest childhood, Florence Nightingale was reared in an atmosphere of 19th century Victorian upper-middle-class privilege and luxury. She and her older sister were born in Italy where her parents had gone for an extended visit after their marriage.

Florence was born May 12, 1820, and was named after her birthplace; her sister was born a year earlier in Naples and was given the Greek name for that city, Parthenope. The girls were educated at home by tutors, governesses, and their father, who personally supervised the whole process of his daughters' schooling. Florence was the better student and excelled in modern and classical languages as well as in many other subjects including history, philosophy, science, music, art, and mathematics.

The developing interests of the two sisters were clearly different. Parthenope (or Parthe) was essentially a conformist who participated willingly in the social and domestic activities that filled the lives of well-to-do young women in high society. Florence, on the other hand, was restless and discontented with the life of the "idle rich" and was often at odds with her mother and sister because she did not live up to their expectations. Mrs. Nightingale and Parthe were not pleased when it became clear that Florence seriously intended to take up nursing, but by that time, Florence had developed a circle of friends who, along with her father, were supportive of her goals (Monteiro, 1990). In 1851, while her mother and sister stayed in Carlsbad (a famous spa in the region of West Bohemia), Florence studied nursing with the deaconesses at the Kaiserswerth Institute in Germany. In 1853, friends were instrumental in helping Nightingale get established at her first job in nursing as the Superintendent of the Harley Street Nursing Home.

In the following year, England entered the Crimean War, and reports about the horrible conditions on the battlefront began to reach London. There was a public outcry demanding nursing care for the sick and wounded soldiers, and Florence Nightingale was asked by the government to organize a nursing staff to go to the war area where she would take charge of providing this care. Nightingale encountered overwhelming obstacles, not the least of which was the intransigence and inefficiency of the military medical establishment, which looked upon her as an interloper. She was, however, endowed with a strong will and determination and, moreover, had influential friends in positions of power. In the end, she prevailed, and when newspaper accounts of her achievements were disseminated at home, she was widely acclaimed as a heroine by a grateful nation upon her return to England in 1856. A fund established in her honor was used to create a nursing school at St. Thomas' Hospital in London.

Much has been written about Florence Nightingale and the complexities of her life. Through her writings and creative genius she is universally known and recognized as the founder of modern nursing. This, however, was not the main or only thrust of her life's work. She made significant contributions to public health, hospital administration, sanitation, and statistics. She served as the uncompromising advocate for the common soldier, and she brought about reforms in the British Army Medical Corps. Nightingale also developed a badly needed cost-accounting system for the British army that was successfully used over a long period. She played a determining role in influencing health legislation in England as well as in India, and she was directly and indirectly involved in many other major reform efforts during her lifetime.

Florence Nightingale was, of course, internationally acclaimed for the reforms she initiated in nursing through which she inspired an atmosphere of dignity and self-respect. Although she was personally motivated by devout religious feelings and a conviction that she had a "calling" from God, she did not seek to perpetuate the image of the self-sacrificing sister of charity that was then fixed in the public mind. She promoted a different kind of nursing career—one in which the nurse would be viewed as a trained, efficient, responsible professional person who would be well paid (Benson & McDevitt, 1980).

Among the numerous biographical, historical, and belletristic works about Florence Nightingale that have been written over the years, one that stands the test of time is Sir Edward Cook's *The Life of Florence Nightingale,* published by Macmillan & Co. in two volumes, 1913-1914. As Nightingale's official biographer, Cook offered a balanced and thorough analysis of her life (Roberts & Group, 1995). Earlier works often treated her with words of adulation and flowery praise and created the legend of *Santa Filomena,* "The Lady with the Lamp" (Longfellow Poems, n.d., pp. 375-376). Not all of her biographers had kind words for her (Smith, 1982; Strachey, 1918), but even one of her most baleful biographers had to admit, albeit grudgingly, that she was a brilliant reformer. He went on to point out that thousands of men in the British army at home and abroad lived healthier, longer lives in better conditions because she had "acted the bully" for them (Benson, 1991).

Recent publications from the field of women's studies have shed new light from a feminist perspective on her life and on the times in which she lived. One of the most moving pieces about her from this genre is a poem by Eleanor Ross Taylor, *Welcome Eumenides*

(Taylor, 1972). The poet uses Nightingale's own words to portray her as a strong, determined, driven woman who defied convention and endured a long personal struggle to follow her destiny, bring order out of chaos, and protect and guard those who needed help. Taylor gives us a stark, moving, and dramatic replay of the frustrations and hardships that were endured by Nightingale in accomplishing her life's mission (Benson, 1993).

With the advent of the Nightingale reforms in the late 19th century, the creation of modern, secular nursing as a profession was followed by rapid expansion and consolidation both in Great Britain and the United States. By the end of the century, just a few decades after the opening of the first school of modern nursing in England, the credibility of nursing had been established, and knowledgeable, trained nurses were greatly in demand. The nursing profession was very appealing to the growing numbers of women of that era, including Jewish women, who were looking for a career outside the home and family.

Summary

In this chapter, we have traversed the 19th century, which witnessed the dawning of a new era for Jews, for women, and for nursing. We picked up the connecting threads among these three entities in order to identify and describe Jewish elements in the annals of nursing history. We also briefly covered some highlights from the life of Florence Nightingale to illustrate her profound influence on the emergence of modern, secular nursing. In so doing, we have set the stage to portray the Jewish heritage in the continuing saga of nursing as it unfolded in 20th century America, the "Golden Land" that held out so much hope for Eastern Europe's Jews.

References

Benson, E. R. (1990). Nineteenth century women, the neophyte nursing profession, and the world's Columbian exposition of 1893. In V. L. Bullough, B. Bullough, & M. P. Stanton (Eds.), *Florence Nightingale and her era: A collection of new scholarship.* New York: Garland Publishing.

Benson, E. R. (1991). Some thoughts on F.B. Smith's Florence Nightingale: Reputationand power. *Bulletin of the American Association for the History of Nursing, 29,* 6-7.

Benson, E. R. (1993). Florence Nightingale in verse. *Pennsylvania Nurse, 48 (5)*,14-15.

Benson, E. R. (1995). Nursing in Germany. *Nursing History Review, 3,*189-200.

Benson E. R., & McDevitt, J. Q. (1980). *Community health and nursing practice* (2nd ed.). Englewood Cliffs, NJ: Prentice-Hall.

Benson, E. R. , & Selekman, J. (1992). Jewish women and nursing: An overview of early history. *Journal of the New York State Nurses Association, 23*(4), 16-19.

Cohen, M. M. (1883). Jewish working-girls. *Jewish Messenger, 53*(1), 4.

Cook, E. (1942). *The life of Florence Nightingale. Vol. 1.* New York: Macmillan.

Dubnow, S. (1975). *History of the Jews in Russia and Poland, from the earliest times until the present day.* New York: KTAV Publishing House.

Fink, G. (1978). *Great Jewish women.* New York: Menorah Publishing.

Florence Nightingale at Harley Street. Her reports to the governors of her nursing home 1853-54. (1970). London: Dent.

Glanz, R. (1976). The Jewish woman in America: Two female immigrant generations 1820-1929. *The Eastern European Jewish woman. Vol. 1.* New York, NY: KTAV Publishing House.

Hebert, R. (1981). *Florence Nightingale: Saint, reformer, or rebel.* Malabar, FL: Robert E. Krieger.

Henry S., & Taitz, E. (1978). *Written out of history: A hidden legacy of Jewish women revealed through their writings and letters.* New York: Block Publishing.

Important exhibitions. (1898, February). *The American Jewess,* p. 242.

Kaplan, M. (1991). *The making of the Jewish middle class: Women, family, and identity in imperial Germany.* New York: Oxford University Press.

Key, E. (1913). *Rahel Varnhagen.* New York: Putnam.

Levin, A. L. (1972). *Dare to be different: A biography of Louis H. Levin of Baltimore.* New York: Bloch Publishing.

Lindenmeyr, A. (1993, Spring). Public life, private virtues: Women in Russian charity, 1762-1914. *Signs,* pp. 562-591.

Longfellow poems. (n.d.). New York: Dutton.

Mayer, S. L. A. (1996). *The Jewish experience in nursing in America: 1881 to 1955.* (Doctoral Dissertation, p. 38). Ann Arbor, MI: University Microfilms International.

Michael Reese Hospital. (1895, October). *The American Jewess,* p. 28.

Monteiro, L. (1990). Nightingale and her correspondents: Portrait of the era. In V. L. Bullough, B. Bullough, & M. P. Stanton, *Florence Nightingale and her era: A collection of new scholarship.* New York: Garland Publishing.

Parsons, M. E. (1983). Mothers and matrons. *Nursing Outlook,* 31, 25-29.

Roberts, J. I., & Group, T. M. (1995). *Feminism and nursing.* Westport, CT: Praeger.

Roth, C. (1970). *A history of the Jews, from earliest times through the six day war.* New York: Schocken Books.

Smith, F. B. (1982). *Florence Nightingale: Reputation and power.* New York: St. Martin's Press.

Sokoloff, L. (1992). A history of Jewish attitudes toward nursing. *New York State Journal of Medicine, 92,* 529-536.

Strachey, L. (1918). *Eminent Victorians.* New York: Putnam.

Taylor, E. R. (1972). *Welcome Eumenides.* New York: George Braziller.

The trained nurse. (1898, April). *The American Jewess,* p. 33.

Where woman reigns supreme (1895, December). *The American Jewess,* pp. 164-166.

Winkler, G. (1991). *They called her Rebbe, the maiden of Ludomir.* New York: Judaica Press.

Wolf, E., & Whiteman, M. (1975). *The history of the Jews of Philadelphia from colonial times to the age of Jackson.* Philadelphia: The Jewish Publication Society of America.

4

In The Golden Land:
Forging Ahead into
The 20th Century

The World's Columbian Exposition:
A Celebration of Women and Nursing

*A*t the close of the 19th century, when older nations still looked upon the United States as an "experiment," the country went all out to stage a spectacular international fair in commemoration of the 400th anniversary of Christopher Columbus' voyage to the New World. The planners viewed this exposition as a unique opportunity to celebrate the nation's democracy, to establish America's credibility before the world community, to debunk myths about the country's cultural inferiority, and to foster patriotism in a period of growing internal unrest. Exceeding the most extravagant expectations of its organizers, the World's Columbian Exposition, or Chicago World's Fair of 1893, was regarded as the crowning cultural event of 19th century America.

Near Lake Michigan arose a majestic "White City" consisting of 150 buildings of Romanesque, Greek, and Renaissance architecture constructed of staff (a material used in putting up temporary buildings). From May through October more than 21 million people paid a 50-cent admission charge to look and marvel at the latest technical achievements such as electric lights, Pullman cars, and the first Ferris wheel. However, this grandiose international event had its shortcomings and negative aspects. With its elaborate facades and ostentatious displays, the fair camouflaged serious ills existing in the community—urban squalor, widespread poverty, human misery, and ugly racism. When the World's Fair was over, all but one of the buildings of this magnificent "White City" were dismantled.

The fair handed down two positive legacies—it organized a series of international congresses and it celebrated women. The 224 congresses were conducted on various subjects including agriculture, religion, and women's progress—and had an estimated attendance of 700,000. The proceedings embodied the ideals that engineered the progressive reform initiatives of early 20th century America.

Notable among these congresses were:

1. The Jewish Women's Congress, which was conducted under the aegis of the Parliament of Religions.

2. The International Congress of Charities, Corrections, and Philanthropy, which sponsored a section on Hospitals, Dispensaries, and Nursing (Benson, 1986).

For the first time at an international exposition, women, including Jewish women and women in nursing, played a conspicuous and prominent role.

- One major outgrowth of the Jewish Women's Congress was the formation of the National Council of Jewish Women, which sought to unite Jewish women for the advancement of religion, philanthropy, and education (Antler, 1997). Since it was established, the National Council of Jewish Women has initiated and supported many worthy community projects, including visiting nurse services and other health care programs.

- The Nursing Congress, which was organized under the International Congress of Charities, Corrections, and Philanthropy, served as an effective public platform from which a group of outstanding leaders set standards for the neophyte profession. Many 20th century goals that were set for nursing education, nursing organization, and nursing administration were conceived and first publicized at this international forum.

Early 20th Century Social and Demographic Changes- Women and Reform

The early part of the 20th century was an era of growth and consolidation in nursing, set against the backdrop of profound military, social, economic, and demographic forces that would shape the future destiny of the United States. Military-wise, the Spanish-American War had recently been terminated. The nation had gone to war with Spain over the issue of Cuba's drive for independence. After the war was over, Cuba had gained its independence, and the United States not only had acquired Guam, Puerto Rico, and the Philippine Islands, but also had achieved international status as a world power to be reckoned with. It was during the Spanish-American War that American nursing had established its place in the military.

People from all walks of life in the early 1900s had to meet the demands of a new and challenging era characterized by rapid and unrelenting shifts in social, economic, and demographic conditions. The social and economic turmoil of those years was fueled by industrial expansion, mass communication, and rapid technologic advances. Demographic changes were driven by a population growth with a massive influx of immigrants and a concentration of people in the cities. Most of the immigrants settled in cities, which, by 1900, held over one-third of the population. By comparison, in 1860, only one-sixth of the nation's population was living in communities with a census of 8,000 or more (Benson, 1993a).

The immigrants of this era were different from earlier groups of immigrants. Most of these newcomers came from Eastern and Southern Europe, rather than from Northern and Western Europe. Between 1900 and 1914, 13 million immigrants entered the United States, and many of them went to work immediately in the burgeoning industries of the country. The presence of these numerous new ethnic minority peoples brought a wide cultural diversity to the United States. The newcomers did not look, sound, or worship like "mainstream" Americans, and sometimes they were viewed with disdain or were regarded as dangerous agitators and radicals. For the most part, however, their basic goal was to become Americanized as quickly as possible and to partake of their share in "the American dream."

This was an era that was ripe for reform—an era that was characterized by a spirit of "rugged individualism," which stemmed from the popular philosophy of social Darwinism. The Darwinian doctrine was one of "survival of the fittest"; the hardest hit were the most vulnerable segments of the population. The prevailing ideology was that government had no responsibility for the welfare of its individual citizens (Sochen, 1974). This was also the era of the so-called "New Woman," a term coined by Henry James referring to privileged American women who scorned social conventions, especially those pertaining to women (Smith-Rosenberg, 1985). The term came to include all women who demanded the rights and privileges that had always been granted only to men. The New Woman sought independence and fulfillment through the pursuit of rewarding work in the public arena.

Reform efforts were being spurred on by private citizens joining forces to express outrage at the injustices of society, and many women stepped into the forefront of such groups. These citizens devoted themselves to humanitarian causes and sought methods to improve the welfare of their fellow human beings. Among them was a whole generation of dynamic women—nurses and non-nurses, Jewish and non-Jewish—who were ardent pioneers in addressing human needs and advancing women's rights. For example, Jane Addams, Lavinia Dock, Josephine Goldmark, Alice Hamilton, Florence Kelley, Julia Lathrop, Henrietta Szold, Lillian Wald, and many others played prominent roles in the major social and political reform movements of the early 20th century.

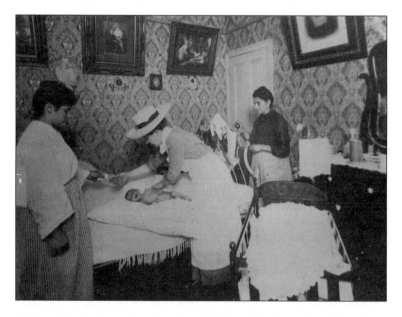

Visiting nurse in home of an immigrant family at the turn of the 20th century.

Courtesy of the Visiting Nurse Society of Philadelphia

The Neophyte Nursing Profession and Its Leaders

In the midst of all of this turmoil, the neophyte nursing profession was making its mark on society. At its helm was a group of remarkable women who contributed to the growth and development of this emerging field as a desirable career choice for women.

Lavinia Dock was an idealist, activist, internationalist who was acknowledged as the profession's first historian. Annie Goodrich played a leading role in local, state, national, and international nursing affairs, and she was appointed dean of the nursing program at Yale University. Mary Eliza Mahoney was the first recognized leader among African American nurses. Mary Adelaide Nutting contributed significantly to the advancement of nursing education and was the first nurse ever appointed to a university professorship. Sophia Palmer and Mary Davis were instrumental in launching the *American Journal of Nursing*. Isabel Hampton Robb was the universally admired leader around whom all others rallied in organizing at the national level. Isabel Stewart spearheaded the development of nursing school curricula and nursing research. Julia Stimson became Superintendent of the Army Nurse Corps in 1900 and also served as Chief Nurse of the American Red Cross. Lillian Wald, a Jewish nurse, was the creative genius who championed social reform and promoted nursing as a community health service (ANA, 1982).

Even in the popular literature of the day, as in, for example, the writings of Dorothy Canfield Fisher, we find an exemplary image of nursing that would appeal to many young women seeking independence and a satisfying career (Benson, 1990a). The profession was developing rapidly and an ever-increasing demand existed for "trained nurses." Anna Fillmore pointed out that in 1900 about 11,000 "trained nurses" existed in the United States and that "a period of dizzy expansion had just begun" (Fillmore, 1941, pp. 913-915). Most of them worked as private duty nurses in homes or as hospital employees. Meanwhile, some found rewarding work as visiting nurses in communities outside of hospital settings.

The Rise of Visiting Nursing and the Henry Street Settlement

In towns and cities throughout the country, visiting nurse services were being established. In many communities, Jewish women played a leading role in organizing these services. For example, in Pittsburgh, the National Council of Jewish Women set up a visiting nurse program in the early 1900s (Selavan, 1980). Louise Waterman Wise, the wife of the eminent Rabbi Stephen S. Wise, was one of the founding members of the Portland, Ore., Visiting Nurse Association in 1902, and she served as its first president (Twenty Years, n.d). Fannie Sax Long spearheaded the formation of the Visiting Nurse Association of Wilkes-Barre, Pa. (Levin,

1999). And perhaps most notable of all was the visiting nurse service or Nurses' Settlement of Henry Street in New York, initiated by Lillian Wald and her colleague, Mary Brewster.

Settlement houses had begun to appear in deprived neighborhoods at the end of the 19th century. They typically provided a variety of community services in a geographically defined area to all residents, irrespective of race, class, national origin, or religion. The Henry Street Settlement House in New York was an extension of Wald and Brewster's nursing project, which, from the outset, was established for the "sick poor." One observer has noted that this was "the first American institution conceived and administered by a trained nurse" (Silverstein, 1985. p. 1). Wald and Brewster's aim was to provide nursing and health care for the impoverished immigrants who had settled in the east-side slums of New York. In their program, these nurses wanted to avoid the stigma of "charity," and so they issued a request that patients pay whatever they could for services whenever possible (Bullough, 1984).

The Jewish Immigrant Population:
Jewish Immigrant Women and Nursing

Among the millions of newly arrived immigrants were many poor Jews from Eastern Europe who were fleeing the tyranny and pogroms of czarist Russia. Like their Spanish-Portuguese and German counterparts who had arrived earlier, they came to this country in search of religious freedom, political liberty, and socioeconomic improvement. Their goal was to enter mainstream American life as quickly as possible. Most of them settled in the large eastern cities, but some made their way to the South and West to smaller communities where they set down roots (Benson & Selekman, 1992). Others chose to live in agricultural settlements, which had been established in various parts of the country specifically for Jewish immigrants as a means to draw them "back to the land" and away from the city.

The immigrant Jewish women of that era found in America a degree of freedom to engage in public life that had not existed in their countries of origin (Benson, 1994). Among the overall immigrant population, it was the young Jewish women who were most eager to become Americanized and to take advantage of the opportunities now available. However, in their quest for independence, they had to cope with daunting obstacles—for example, despite their new-found freedom, they had to face an American community that did not altogether approve of career women and that sometimes looked down on them as Jews. They also had to come to grips with a 3,000-year-old tradition that expected Jewish women to stay at home and care for their husbands and children.

In time, some of these women began to seek careers in nursing and social work. As mentioned earlier, nursing was coming into its own and had a broad appeal to women who sought independence and personal fulfillment. With the establishment of training schools in Jewish hospitals, recruitment efforts were directed at the Jewish community. The Jewish press had already begun to promote nursing as a career for young immigrant Jewish women (see *The American Jewess*, 1895, 1898; Cohen, 1883; Glanz, 1976). At the same time, the Jewish press and other sources had also acknowledged a prevailing negative attitude in the Jewish community as follows:

- The author of an article in *The American Jewess*, promoting nursing for Jewish women, expressed puzzlement over the fact that "Jewish women have been slow in possessing themselves of a calling for which they are eminently fitted" and lamented the "false prejudices and parental objections" that deprived the nursing profession of a corps of potentially superb candidates (Where Woman Reigns Supreme, 1895, pp. 164-166).

- Rabbi Samuel Sale, when addressing a gathering of nurses at the 17th annual convention of the American Nurses' Association in 1914, referred to the sacred duty of the Jews "to tend and nurse the sick" and alluded to the fact that Jewish nurses were probably underrepresented in the ranks of nursing (Sale, 1914).

- Another article indicated that "the Jews . . . have been among the last to overcome the old-fashioned prejudice against nursing, and until recently entering a career of nursing was regarded almost the same as entering a convent or becoming a domestic servant" (Linenthal, 1990, pp. 134-135).

Concerning the allusion to the convent, it should be noted that, throughout this era, nursing textbooks often emphasized the connection between nursing and Christianity. A typical example appears in an early public health nursing textbook, which stated that "the work of the public health nurse is founded in Christian charity" and "district nursing is as old as the Christian Church" (Brainard, 1985, pp. 420; 102).

By the early 20th century, however, young Jewish women were coming into the nursing profession. Rebekah Kohut wrote a fascinating account of the Jewish immigrant experience, in which she described life in the ghetto and the achievements of those who emerged from its midst in one generation, as follows:

> There was misery and squalor there; misery and squalor as pitiful as that in the ghettos of Russia. But there was a new hope, a new eagerness, a new confidence. The shadow of Czarist oppression had vanished. In the light of American opportunity the future seemed—whatever man's dreams could make of it. . . . Cantors' sons, full of the music which permeated their homes, became American composers and singers. The sons of rabbis became actors and prize fighters, lawyers and journalists. Tailors' sons and daughters became teachers. . . . Their cousin, who had a newspaper route, wound up in a university chair of philosophy. They had a mutual second cousin . . . at the head of a training school for nurses (Kohut, 1929, p. 2).

It would appear that, for the most part, Jewish women chose to enter Jewish hospital training schools. It has been noted that the nursing schools of Bellevue Hospital and the New York Hospital together had graduated only four Jewish students from 1875-1920 (Mottus, 1981). Whether Jewish candidates felt more comfortable in an institution with a Jewish connection or whether they were excluded from other schools is not known for certain (Linenthal, 1990). To be sure, the Jewish hospital training schools, which were nonsectarian, also admitted many non-Jewish students. Thus, for example, in 1903 at the Jewish Hospital School of Nursing in Philadelphia, 26 nursing students were enrolled, and about two-thirds of them were non-Jewish (Whiteman, 1966).

Lillian Wald, mid-1930s

In front of banner designed for her trip to China and Japan, 1910. "Wald had noticed that Chinese family members all wore the same insignia on their clothing. She wanted an insignia for the Henry Street nurses that would signify 'we are all one family'. This insignia was developed by a Japanese artist from Chinese symbols. They have been translated to mean universal brotherhood." (From personal correspondence with Sari Weintraub, Development Assistant, Henry Street Settlement, May 9, 2000.)
Courtesy of Louise Schafer, RN (deceased), a public health nursing executive, who served in the 1930s on the staff of the Visiting Nurse Service in New York.

Jewish Hospitals and Jewish Community Support
for Health and Social Welfare Programs

Within the organizational structure of the Jewish hospitals, the women's committees were often the ones who prodded administrators into establishing and maintaining nurses' training schools. For example, Rose Frank of Philadelphia was instrumental in establishing the nursing school at the Jewish Hospital in Philadelphia in 1892, and Maud Nathan, one of New York's leading progressive social reformers of the early 20th century, was active in the Mt. Sinai Hospital School of Nursing in New York (Benson & Selekman, 1992). These women and many of their peers devoted their energy and resources to the organization of nurses' training schools in hospitals that were established by Jewish communities throughout the country during this period.

Many other nursing, health, and welfare programs to aid the large numbers of poverty stricken immigrants, both Jewish and non-Jewish, were undertaken and supported by members of the Jewish community in early 20th century America. The Spanish-Portuguese and German Jews who made up the bulk of the earlier Jewish immigrations to the United States were, by this time, essentially integrated and well established. To some extent, they may have joined mainstream American society in looking down on the East European newcomers as "foreigners." However, a highly developed sense of community responsibility existed within the established Jewish population group, and when called upon for help, they responded generously with time and money—contributing to numerous projects designed to promote public health and social welfare.

These contributors mostly came from the well-to-do, successful, and largely integrated German-Jewish community of the early 20th century. For example, Jacob Schiff, a leading financier and one of the greatest philanthropists of that time, was a principal supporter of Lillian Wald in her work at the Henry Street Settlement. Schiff was also a major contributor to the public health nursing programs of the Red Cross Town and Country Nursing Service, which flourished in the early years of the 20th century. Schiff was a staunch believer in the Judaic precept of *tzedaqa*, or "righteous giving," which is not only charity but also a civic responsibility. With regard to his generous support of nursing, health, and social services, Schiff labeled the "survival of the fittest" ideology as a cruelty and wrote, ". . . we should feel that duty calls us to step in and be of help to those who are left behind" (Daniels, 1989, p. 37).

The Jewish community was blessed with many other generous benefactors whose support was not restricted to their fellow Jews. Among the group, we find, for example, Felix Adler, founder of the Ethical Culture Society, who, as a member of the Tenement House Commission, was instrumental in sending visiting nurses to help poor immigrant tenants in their homes. Nathan Straus was active in the campaign for the production and distribution of pasteurized milk, and he established stations where safe milk supplies could be obtained. Simon Guggenheim, who served as a U.S. Senator from Colorado, gave his support to establishing the Children's Bureau in 1912, in which Lillian Wald played a pivotal role (Benson, 1993b).

Lillian Wald, 1867-1940, Public Health Nurse

In the annals of nursing history, Lillian Wald (1867-1940) stands out as a towering figure of strength, creativity, and practical idealism. Because Wald is so closely associated with social reform, many sources, especially Jewish sources, persist in identifying her as a social worker, rather than as a nurse, on the assumption that nursing and social reform do not go together—a point that rankles nurses. However, Wald was first and foremost a nurse, and within the context of a work on Jewish women in nursing, she comes to mind before all others. Like Florence Nightingale, Wald came from a highly cultured, upper-middle-class family who did not altogether approve of her becoming a nurse.

Wald was born in Cincinnati, Ohio, in 1867, to Max D. and Minnie Schwarz Wald, who were German-Jewish immigrants. They moved from Cincinnati to Dayton and then to Rochester, N.Y., where Lillian grew up in the midst of a loving, close-knit family. She was educated in a private school in Rochester, and when she was 16 years old, she applied for admission to Vassar but was not accepted because of her age. She stayed at home and tried to enjoy the pleasant life of a young woman in a well-to-do socially active family. But, she became restless and wanted to get out into the world and do something more meaningful. She found herself irresistibly drawn to the newly created profession of nursing after she had observed the "trained nurse" who was brought in to care for her sister. In 1889, Wald entered the New York Hospital School of Nursing, which for many years had graduated virtually no Jewish students.

After completing her nursing program and working for a brief period, Wald decided to go to medical school. Soon after she had begun her studies there, she agreed to teach a class in home nursing to immigrants on the Lower East Side. One day, during class, a child came up to her and said that Wald's help was needed at the child's home. Wald went with the child to a run-down tenement where she found the child's mother lying gravely ill in the midst of abject poverty and destitution. Coming face-to-face so dramatically with the grim reality of the social and economic deprivation in the neighborhood, Wald experienced what she called a "baptism of fire" (Wald, 1971, p. 7) that drove her out of medical school and into a life of service in the slums. She went to live in that area, and, in time, she and her colleague, Mary Brewster, moved to Henry Street where they set up the Nurses' Settlement to provide nursing services to the community.

A passionate and dedicated social reformer, Wald linked nursing with the women's movement and was a staunch advocate of the nursing profession—in her words, ". . . skillful nursing is of greater value in preserving human life than the best medical advice" (Daniels, 1989, p. 28). Wald, who coined the term "public health nursing," has been characterized as the "creative shaper" of that field of nursing (Buhler-Wilkerson, 1989, p. 18). She played a prominent role in many of the social causes of that era. Universalist in her outlook, Wald was a secular rather than a religious Jew. Nevertheless, she maintained strong ties with members of the Jewish community from whom she obtained much of the financial support that she needed for her life's work (Benson, 1993b).

Wald's projects were beacons of hope and inspiration to the teeming masses of immigrants in the slums of New York's East Side. "Miss Wald comes to our house, and a new world opens for us. We recommend to her all our neighbours who are in need. The children join clubs in the Nurses' Settlement and I spend a great deal of time there. Miss Wald and Miss Brewster treat me with affectionate kindness" (Cohen, 1918, p. 231). These are the words of a young Jewish immigrant who came to this country, took a job in a tenement sweatshop, and when she was laid off, went to work as a servant and later as a worker in a garment shop. She attended night school to study English, checked out books from the free library, and was encouraged by an instructor to write a personal memoir about the immigrant experience. She wrote her autobiography wherein she expressed admiration for the nurses at Henry Street, and especially for Lillian Wald who came to her home to take care of her when she became ill (Cohen, 1918/1995).

In establishing the Nurses' Settlement and the Henry Street Settlement House, Lillian Wald attracted many loyal followers, Jews as well as non-Jews. One of her most highly respected colleagues and staunchest admirers was Lavinia Dock, eminent leader and historian of nursing. Dock, who came from a liberal, Christian background, joined the Visiting Nurses of the Henry Street Settlement House to work as a public health nurse among the immigrant population on the Lower East Side. A political activist with radical opinions, Dock soon felt a kinship with Jewish immigrants. She identified with them in "their lifelong ideals for a better life for all humanity and their struggles and their persecution in the Labor Movement" (Dock, 1977, p. 25). Dock singled out these immigrants for their "intellectual, moral, and spiritual penetration and perceptions" and she characterized them as "intellectual and idealistic . . . of international outlook and sympathies . . . the highest type of civilized [humans]" (p. 25). She believed that all of these qualities were exemplified by Lillian Wald whose "nature seemed . . . to surpass any other . . . [and] like the sun, she radiated her beams on all without demands or exactions for a return" (p. 25).

Wald inspired all who were concerned about their fellow human beings. For example, Herbert Lehman, born of a well-established German-Jewish family in New York City, who in his later years served as the Governor of New York and as a U.S. Senator, attributed his humanitarianism to Lillian Wald, under whose influence he had joined the Henry Street Settlement. Wald was a source of inspiration to many of the independent women of that era who were entering public life. For example, spurred on by Wald's visiting nurse scheme, Henrietta Szold, the great 20th century humanitarian and Zionist leader, who was not a nurse, came to recognize public health nursing as the means of providing primary health care, which she used as the basis for her pioneering work in Palestine.

Henrietta Szold (1860-1945): Zionist Pioneer, Promoter of Nursing and Health Care

An activist, teacher, writer, and champion of women's emancipation, Henrietta Szold (1860-1945), the founder of the Women's Zionist Organization of Hadassah, was born in Baltimore, the eldest child of Sophie and Rabbi Benjamin Szold. Her parents had migrated from Hungary to America in 1859, when her father was

Henrietta Szold

Source: Nachum T. Gidal, *Henrietta Szold: The Saga of an American Woman.* Jerusalem: Gefen Publishing House, 1997. Courtesy of Pia Gidal.

called to serve as rabbi of the new congregation, Oheb Shalom, in Baltimore. Szold, who grew up in an intellectually stimulating atmosphere, was a brilliant and serious student, having mastered several languages at an early age. She worked with her father as his research assistant and also taught in a small private school—in addition, she wrote essays for a Jewish newspaper in New York. When she was 21, she toured the great European cultural centers with her father, who went back to visit relatives.

Upon her return to Baltimore, she worked with many Russian-Jewish immigrants to help them settle into mainstream America. She found these poor, struggling newcomers to be intellectually stimulating, and she was in total harmony with their progressive ideals and Zionist aspirations. She helped to establish the Russian

Rachel Landy (left) and **Rose Kaplan** (right)

The first American nurses sent by Hadassah to Jerusalem, 1913, with Eva Leon (center), a member of the New York chapter. Outside the original Nurses Settlement.
Source: Hadassah Archives.

Night School, where she served as teacher and principal. Her commitment to Zionism grew stronger, and she considered it to be the essential element of Judaism at that time. She continued writing for various publications, and she acquired a reputation as a "leading Jewish essayist in America" (Benson, 1990b, p. 4).

After her father died in 1902, she and her mother moved to New York where Szold was admitted to the Jewish Theological Seminary, which was a radical step for the institution; at that time no women were studying at rabbinical seminaries. This period of her life ended painfully in her late 40s when one of her colleagues, a man nearly 14 years younger to whom she had been deeply devoted personally and professionally, announced his intention to marry a young woman from Vienna. Szold left the seminary and with her elderly mother took a long and arduous journey through Europe and the Middle East. In Palestine she saw dreadful poverty, disease, and suffering among the Jewish settlers, and she knew something had to be done. Her family was hoping that a visit to Palestine would extinguish her Zionist fervor. But that did not happen, and, even before she returned home in 1910, she was more convinced than ever that Zionism was the key to the survival of the Jewish people.

Hadassah and Public Health Nursing in Action: Rose Kaplan and Rachel (Rae) Landy

In 1912, Szold launched her organization, The Daughters of Zion—Hadassah Chapter. Her goal to create a public health nursing service based on Lillian Wald's model at Henry Street received no support from the organized Zionist establishment in the United States or Palestine. But this did not stop her. She mobilized Hadassah members to raise money for the project. Some contributions came in from other members of the Jewish community. A most generous benefactor was Nathan Straus, the great philanthropist and public health advocate.

Szold recruited two Jewish nurses, Rose Kaplan and Rae Landy, who had been working in New York hospitals. In 1913, just before World War I, Kaplan and Landy sailed for Palestine with Mr. and Mrs. Nathan Straus. In Jerusalem, they posted a sign outside their house in Hebrew and English: AMERICAN DAUGHTERS OF ZION NURSES SETTLEMENT HADASSAH, which became a nurse-managed public health center. From the beginning, Kaplan and Landy were beset by monumental difficulties.

Among the extremely poor inhabitants living in filthy conditions, the nurses found severely malnourished infants, children whose eyelids were encrusted with flies, desperately sick people suffering from diseases such as cholera, dysentery, malaria, and typhoid fever. Of utmost concern to the nurses was the high maternal mortality rate that was related to poor hygienic practices of untrained midwives. In addition, Kaplan and Landy were looked upon with suspicion—most nurses who went to Jerusalem in those days were nuns, whose goals included religious conversion of the local population.

Undaunted, the two nurses attacked the major problems; they worked hard and were often lonely. Within a year they had begun their district nursing service, trained women to help in their home visits, organized a midwife service, and were successful in the fight against trachoma through treatment in schools and home visits. The nurses kept in touch with their professional colleagues in the United States who were eager to learn of their progress. A report they sent from Palestine to the 17th annual convention of the American Nurses' Association in St. Louis, Missouri, appeared in the Proceedings of the Convention April 23-29, 1914, published in the *American Journal of Nursing* (Benson, 1990b).

Unfortunately their public health nursing scheme was interrupted by the outbreak of World War I in 1914. Palestine was in a state of upheaval and the situation deteriorated rapidly. Nevertheless, the accomplishments of Kaplan and Landy were not forgotten, and they served as an inspiration for the nursing programs later established by Hadassah, for example, the maternity welfare centers, a School Hygiene Service, and, especially, the School of Nursing—which opened in 1918. The first class of nurses was graduated in 1921 (Bartal & Steiner-Freud, 1999). In fact, at that time, these Hadassah-sponsored nursing projects became a model for neighboring areas such as Transjordan, Egypt, and the Isle of Rhodes.

Summary

This chapter has traced the progress of nursing in early 20th century America and has shown how young Jewish immigrant women were encouraged to enter the nursing profession. The Jewish press was very supportive of the nursing profession and tried to counteract what was perceived as a negative view in the Jewish community. Despite many obstacles, tangible and intangible, young Jewish women enrolled in nursing schools and went on to have rewarding and successful careers.

Throughout this period, members of the established Jewish community, who had been integrated into mainstream American life, were generous benefactors in promoting social causes. The Jewish community and Jewish women of the early 20th century made a significant contribution to the continued growth and development of the nursing profession and to many other related health, social, and welfare programs.

Many Jewish women played an activist role in social reform movements of that era, and one in particular—Lillian Wald, a Jewish nurse—was a larger-than-life figure who inspired all who knew her. Wald's public health nursing program served as the impetus to the fulfillment of Henrietta Szold's vision for creating health and social welfare projects in Palestine. It was through the courage and dedication of two American Jewish nurses, Kaplan and Landy, that health care was brought to the poor inhabitants of a distant outpost in the Middle East where the roots for the future Zionist state were planted.

References

ANA (1982). *Nursing hall of fame.* (Booklet G-123 5M 6/82). Washington, DC: Author.

Antler, J. (1997). *The journey home: Jewish women and the American century.* New York: The Free Press.

Bartal, N., & Steiner-Freud, J. (1999). *The first graduating class: Hadassah school of nursing 1921.* New York: Hadassah, The Women's Zionist Organization of America.

Benson, E. (1986). Nursing and the world's Columbian exposition. *Nursing Outlook, 34,* 88-90.

Benson, E. R. (1990a). An early 20th century view of nursing. *Nursing Outlook, 38,* 275-277.

Benson, E. R. (1990b). Hadassah and the nursing connection: Early days. *Bulletin of the American Association for the History of Nursing, 26,* 4-6.

Benson, E. (1993a). Toward social reform, 1894-1913. In N. Birnbach & S. Lewenson (Eds.), *Legacy of leadership.* New York: National League for Nursing.

Benson, E. R. (1993b). Public health nursing and the Jewish contribution. *Public Health Nursing 10,* 55-57.

Benson, E. R. (1994). Jewish nurses: A multicultural perspective. *Journal of the New York State Nurses Association, 25*(2), 8-10.

Benson, E. R., & Selekman, J. (1992). Jewish women and nursing. *Journal of the New York State Nurses Association, 23,* 16-19.

Brainard, A. M. (1985). *The evolution of public health nursing.* New York: Garland.

Buhler-Wilkerson, K. (1989). *False dawn: The rise and decline of Public Health Nursing, 1900-1930.* New York: Garland.

Bullough, B. (1984). Clinical specialization in nursing – Historical overview. In S. Fondiller (Ed.), *Conference proceedings of the American Association for the History of Nursing,* New Orleans, LA: AAHN.

Cohen, M. M. (1883). Jewish working-girls. *Jewish Messenger, 53*(1), 4.

Cohen, R. (1918). *Out of the shadow.* New York: George H. Doran Co. (Reprinted in 1995 with an introduction by Thomas Dublin).

Daniels, D. G. (1989). *Always a sister: The feminism of Lillian D. Wald.* New York: The Feminist Press.

Dock, L. (1977). Self-Portrait. *Nursing Outlook 25,* 22-26.

Fillmore, A. (1941). Scene – USA, 1900. *American Journal of Nursing, 41*(8), 913-915.

Glanz, R. (1976). The Jewish woman in America: Two female immigrant generations 1820-1929. *The Eastern European Jewish woman. Volume I.* New York: KTAV Publishing House.

Kohut, R. (1929). *As I know them.* Garden City, NY: Doubleday, Doran, & Co.

Levin, M. (Ed.). (1999). *The Jews of Wilkes-Barre.* Wilkes-Barre, PA: Jewish Community Center of Wyoming Valley.

Linenthal, A. J. (1990). Jewish advocate. In *First a dream: The history of Boston's Jewish hospitals, 1896-1920.* Boston: Beth Israel Hospital in Association with the Francis A. Countway Library of Medicine.

Mottus, J. E. (1981). *New York Nightingales: The emergence of the nursing profession at Bellevue and New York hospital 1850-1920.* Ann Arbor, MI: UMI-Research Press.

Sale, R. S. (1914). American Nurses' Association proceedings of the 17th annual convention: Nursing work of religious organizations, I. *American Journal of Nursing, 14,* 874-875,

Selavan, I. C. (1980). Angel in hell-with-the-lid-off. *American Journal of Nursing, 80*(11), 2064-2066.

Silverstein, N. G. (1985). Lillian Wald at Henry Street, 1893-1895. *Advances in Nursing Science, 7*(2), 1-12.

Smith-Rosenberg, C. (1985). *Disorderly conduct: Visions of gender in Victorian America.* New York: Alfred A. Knopf.

Sochen, J. (1974). *Herstory – A woman's view of American history.* New York: Alfred Publishing.

Twenty years of the Portland Visiting Nurse Association, 1902-1921. (Pamphlet) (n.d.). Portland, OR: Oregon Health Sciences University Library.

Wald, L. D. (1971). *The house on Henry Street.* New York: Dover.

Where woman reigns supreme. (1895). *The American Jewess,* pp. 164-166.

Whiteman, M. (1966). *Mankind and medicine: A history of Philadelphia's Albert Einstein medical center.* Philadelphia: Albert Einstein Medical Center.

5

 ## "It's *Not* For a Jewish Girl!"
or Is It?
Jewish Role Models
In Early 20th Century Nursing

"$\mathfrak{I}$t's *not* for a Jewish girl!" Such was the response that often greeted a young Jewish woman in years gone by when she expressed her wish to enter nursing school. Among Jewish nurses of a certain age many can probably recall having heard this expression from family members, friends, or acquaintances. It would seem that nursing has not enjoyed the *yichus* (i.e., inherent nobility or distinction) that has been unconditionally associated with the medical profession, especially in the Jewish community. From the earliest times in Scripture and tradition, physicians have occupied an exalted status in the Jewish community and were sometimes regarded as "messengers of God." Not so with nursing.

Throughout history, nursing has been perceived by society as being woman's work and has traditionally been relegated to a subordinate position. To be sure, nursing, from its ascribed connection with the Church and religious orders, achieved a mark of respectability within the non-Jewish community. "Nursing's roots lie in Christianity; nursing is a Christian calling." These were common assertions in popular and professional literature of the early 20th century. Overall, however, even in the non-Jewish community, the professional and communal status of nursing was not considered on a par with that of the medical profession. This point has been underscored by a particular aspect of the feminist mission, which, while seeking to open up new careers to women, seems to say, "Why be a nurse if you can be a doctor?" This message has left an inauspicious imprint on women and on nursing in both the Jewish and the non-Jewish communities, even though, overall, the feminist movement has helped to strengthen a sense of independent identity for nurses (James, 1984). A true mark of success for the feminist cause will be achieved when "traditionally female professions like nursing gain the high value and social support they deserve" (Baer, 1991).

Jewish women in nursing, it would seem, have more than one strike against them. Popular authors, entertainers, and "comedians"—many of them Jewish and bent on wringing "humor" from ethnic stereotypes—have coined obnoxious epithets. They have often succeeded in promoting offensive images that have struck a responsive chord among those who harbor ill feelings toward Jews, especially toward Jewish women. It should come as no surprise that Jewish nurses, at times, have been the target of snide and scornful remarks by some non-Jews within the nursing community. For instance, "Oh, you're Jewish? I always thought that Jewish women don't go into nursing because they're spoiled, they don't want to get their hands dirty."

Thus, for young Jewish women in the first half of the 20th century, the path leading to a career in nursing was not without bumps and detours. "It's not for a Jewish girl!" "Nursing's roots lie in Christianity, nursing is a Christian calling." Inundated with such less-than-inspiring messages, is it any wonder that Jewish women probably did not enter the nursing profession in numbers comparable to their non-Jewish counterparts? Nonetheless, as already discussed (see Chapter 4), there were many Jewish women, undeterred by such sentiments, who became nurses and had very rewarding careers. Some of them even emerged as distinguished leaders of the profession. In addition, other Jewish women, who were not nurses, became valiant advocates and worked tirelessly to promote the development of the profession in its early years.

We have already spoken of Lillian Wald and of her invaluable contribution to nursing and society. However, other notable Jewish women have also contributed to the nursing profession during the first half of the 20th century. Consider, for example, the following women and their achievements.

Margaret Gene Arnstein (1904-1972)

Margaret Gene Arnstein greatly enriched the field of public health nursing in the United States in a career that spanned nearly half a century (Brody, 1996; Fondiller, 1988). One of four children, Arnstein was born in New York into an affluent Jewish family that honored the Jewish tradition. Her parents, Elsie (Nathan) and Leo Arnstein, were 2nd generation Americans from the German-Jewish community who were actively involved in public health and social welfare endeavors. Leo Arnstein served for several years on the board of directors and executive committee of the Henry Street Settlement and was a close friend of Lillian Wald.

As a child, Margaret Arnstein had visited the Henry Street Settlement and, under the influence of Lillian Wald, became interested in public health nursing. After her graduation from Smith College in 1925, Arnstein went on to complete the New York Presbyterian Hospital School of Nursing's 27-month program designed for college graduates. Receiving her diploma in 1928, Arnstein continued her education at Teachers College, Columbia University where she earned the M.A. degree 1 year later. In 1934, Johns Hopkins University awarded her a second master's degree in public health.

Margaret Gene Arnstein, c.1949

Courtesy of the U.S. Department of Health and Human Services, Office of Public Health Service Historian.

Arnstein's career in nursing was launched as a public health staff nurse at the Westchester County Health Department in White Plains, New York. From the early 1930s, until her retirement in 1972, Arnstein brought a vision to the profession through her innovative leadership at national and international levels. For nearly two decades she was associated with the U.S. Public Health Service, aiming to strengthen research in the field of public health nursing. She held a number of academic positions including her last appointment in the late 1960s as Dean of the Yale University School of Nursing. In the fall of 1972, Arnstein announced her retirement from Yale and shortly afterward died.

Esther Silverstein Blanc (1913-1997)

Esther Silverstein Blanc's career in nursing was closely linked to the liberal tradition and noble ideals that permeated her family background. Her parents, Gazella (Kranz) and Simon Huester Silverstein, came from Rumania and were part of that group of Jewish immigrants who were encouraged to go West and settle on farms. The Silversteins moved to Wyoming where, around the towns of Chugwater and Torrington, Baron de Hirsch had established farming communities for immigrant Jewish families. Esther Silverstein Blanc was born in Goshen County, Wyoming, in 1913, one of eight children. All of their neighbors were Eastern European Jewish immigrants who spoke Yiddish and each day awaited the arrival of their copies of the *Forvartz* (the Yiddish language daily newspaper, Forward, from New York).

When Blanc was a young child, she lost her grandmother and older sister to the influenza epidemic of 1918. Two other pivotal events occurred in her life when she was 12 years old. First, she was hospitalized for appendicitis in Cheyenne where she said, "the nurses were great . . . nursing appealed to me." From then on nursing became her chosen career. Second, after a few successive unproductive years on the farm, her family moved to nearby Mitchell, Nebraska, where "we were the only Jewish family in town . . . I used to sing in the Methodist church" (personal communications, Esther Silverstein Blanc, June 4, 1990; Paul Blanc, son of Esther Blanc, April 2000).

Blanc entered nursing school with her family's full support, and in 1934, she earned her diploma in nursing at the University of California (San Francisco) School of Nursing. In 1937, Blanc volunteered to serve in Spain as a nurse with the International Bri-

Esther Silverstein Blanc, c.1938

Courtesy of Mr. Brice Wilkins, Publisher, *The Index*, Mitchell, NE.

gade in their struggle against Fascism during the Spanish Civil War. Most of the nurses with whom she served were Jewish; they came from the United States and from many other countries (personal communication, Esther Silverstein Blanc, June 4, 1990). In her memoir, Blanc wrote about Spain, "Interest in the Spanish civil war was particularly strong among those of us who were Jewish and well aware of what was happening in fascist Germany . . . I felt that I was volunteering for all the Jews all over the world and all the people who were being oppressed by the Nazis and other fascists" (Hayton-Keeva, 1987, pp. 199-200).

In 1938, Blanc was sent home after she contracted malaria, dysentery, and undulant fever. She returned to Mitchell and wrote about her experiences in her hometown newspaper, the *Index*. Blanc moved ahead in nursing, eventually serving in the U.S.

Army Nurse Corps during World War II. Following her discharge from the service, she met her future husband, a research geneticist, in California.

After they were married, Blanc earned her baccalaureate degree in 1946 at the University of Rochester. A few years later, her husband accepted a position at the University of Oklahoma, where they went to live and where their children were born. This portion of Blanc's life coincided with the infamous McCarthy era. Both she and her husband were political progressives, a view that was highly suspect in academia at that time. The vulnerability of their position was compounded by the fact that Esther Blanc had served in Spain with the anti-fascists. Ultimately, her husband was black-listed and forced to give up his university appointment.

The Blancs then made their home in San Francisco, where Esther worked in public health and continued her education, earning her MSN degree in 1961 and her doctorate in the History of Health Sciences in 1972 at the University of California, San Francisco (UCSF). From 1964 through 1967 she taught at the UCSF School of Nursing, and after she completed her doctoral studies, she taught history of medicine for 11 years at the UCSF School of Medicine, retiring in 1984. Following her retirement she found success in an entirely new career as an author of children's stories. Her award-winning story, *Berchick*, about a "Jewish" horse was based on early childhood experiences on her family's homestead in Wyoming. She continued to study and write until her death in April 1997.

Naomi Deutsch (1890-1983)

A towering figure in the field of public health nursing was Naomi Deutsch, born in 1890 in Austria, to Hermine (Bacher) and Rabbi Gotthard Deutsch. Her parents left their native land in 1891 and emigrated to the United States. They made their home in Cincinnati, Ohio, where Rabbi Deutsch had been recruited to serve on the faculty of Hebrew Union College. Naomi was one of five children, growing up in a busy, active household. She finished high school in 1908 and later entered the Jewish Hospital School of Nursing in Cincinnati. After completing nursing school in 1912, Deutsch worked as a public health nurse in Cincinnati and then in Pittsburgh, Pa. She enrolled at Teachers College, Columbia University for advanced study and received a baccalaureate degree in 1921.

For several years, Deutsch served under Lillian Wald with the

Naomi Deutsch.

Henry Street Visiting Nurses. Her next move was to San Francisco in 1925 where she took a position as Director of the Visiting Nurse Association. In 1934, she was appointed Assistant Professor of Public Health Nursing at Berkeley. She was active in the California State Organization for Public Health Nursing and the California State Nurses Association. Deutsch's accomplishments were recognized by prominent nursing leaders throughout the country, including Lillian Wald. In 1935, she was called to Washington where she was appointed director of public health nursing in the U.S. Children's Bureau. Under the provisions of the Social Security Act of 1935, this was a very important position with a lot of responsibility, and Deutsch was considered the best qualified candidate.

In the early 1940s, Deutsch worked with the Pan American Sanitary Bureau in its campaign to develop health programs in the Caribbean and in Central America. She provided leadership in organizing visiting nursing services and in promoting nursing education in that part of the world. Deutsch left government service in 1945 and retired to New York City where she taught part-time for several years at Teachers College, Columbia University. In the early 1970s, she moved to New Orleans to care for her sister, who was in poor health. After her sister's death, Deutsch stayed on in New Orleans; she died in 1983 at the age of 93 (Mayer, 1996; Roberts, 1954).

Emma Goldman (1869-1940)

How, you may ask, does Emma Goldman—anarchist, feminist, supporter of radical causes, advocate of free speech and birth control, lecturer, and writer—come to be counted among notable Jewish women in nursing? Goldman was born in 1869 to Taube (Bienowitch) and Abraham Goldman in Kovno, Russia (now a part of Lithuania). In 1885, Goldman left Russia with her half-sister and emigrated to America. She settled in Rochester, N.Y., and went to work in a clothing factory.

The harshness of her early family life, the injustices of society, the vile anti-Semitism in czarist Russia, and her early contacts with nihilist and populist university students in St. Petersburg drew her into a life of radicalism and anarchy. In 1889, she left Rochester and went to New York City where she became acquainted with a group of radical thinkers. She was caught up in their anarchist movement and in their accompanying acts of violence. In 1893, she was sentenced to one year in prison, where she took up work

photograph by T. Kajiwara

Emma Goldman, c.1900

Labadie Collection,
University of Michigan Library

**Josephine
Goldmark**

Courtesy of
Bryn Mawr
College Library

as a practical nurse. Later, she studied nursing and midwifery in Vienna.

For Goldman, nursing became a means to an end, allowing her to earn money for her public role as a radical political activist. She worked as a nurse and midwife on the Lower East Side, where she was well thought of and highly respected for her competence and capability. Emma Goldman knew and admired Lavinia Dock. Goldman and Lillian Wald were acquainted with each other, but while their relationship was one of mutual trust, they were not really friends. Goldman was not an advocate of settlement work, but she had great respect for Wald and valued her opinion.

Throughout Goldman's extensive travels, her dynamic personality and skill at public speaking drew many people to her cause. After a stormy, tempestuous life that took her to many countries around the world, Goldman died on a trip to Canada in 1940 (Bullough, Church, & Stein, 1988; Daniels, 1989; James, 1971).

Josephine Goldmark (1877-1950)

When we examine the history of nursing in the United States, we find many distinguished women who, though they were not nurses, contributed to the development of the profession through their special expertise. Foremost among these individuals was Josephine Goldmark, the pioneer social researcher whose interest in social legislation and reform brought her into the arena of nursing. Within the nursing community she is best known for her contribution to the landmark study of Nursing and Nursing Education in the United States (1923), often referred to as the *Goldmark Report*. In 1920, Goldmark had also published the results of an extensive health and hospital survey that called attention to the problems of inadequate housing facilities for nursing students. Both of these studies were influential in bringing about improvements in nursing education.

Josephine Goldmark was born in Brooklyn, N.Y., to Regina (Wehle) and Dr. Joseph Goldmark, who were Jewish immigrants from the Austro-Hungarian empire in the aftermath of the Continental Revolutions of 1848. Goldmark's father died when she was only 3 years old, but the family was financially comfortable and she grew up in a culturally and intellectually enriched atmosphere. After receiving her degree in English at Bryn Mawr College, Goldmark attended graduate school at Barnard College.

Josephine Goldmark was influenced by the liberal tradition of her parents and their generation of Jewish immigrants. At the turn of the century, Goldmark began to work as a volunteer with the National Consumers League, which, from the 1890s through the 1930s, fought for the improvement of workers' conditions. Goldmark spearheaded a project on child labor reform and also assisted her brother-in-law, Louis Brandeis, in his efforts to advance progressive social legislation.

From its inception, Goldmark's work brought her into close contact with public health nurses, such as Lavinia Dock, whom she often used as a resource person in her research. Goldmark recognized and appreciated the role of public health nursing in promoting human welfare. She greatly admired Lillian Wald and paid tribute to Wald's innovative nursing service in the community. She served on the Board of Directors of the Henry Street Visiting Nurses Association, and she worked for the advancement of public health nursing. After living in and around New York City for most of her life, Goldmark moved to Hartsdale, N.Y., where she spent her last years with one of her sisters. She died of a heart ailment in 1950 at the age of 73 (Benson 1987; James, 1971).

Amelia Greenwald (1881-1966)

Amelia Greenwald came from an immigrant German-Jewish merchant family who had settled in the southern United States. Greenwald was born in Gainesville, Ala., in 1881, to Elisha (Haas) and Joseph Greenwald. Her father, having served in the Confederate Army during the Civil War, was well-established in his community where he had, for a time, been mayor. In her childhood, Greenwald had listened to her father's stories about nurses in the Civil War, which inspired her to enter nursing (Mayer, 1994; Sokoloff, 1994).

Over her family's objections, Greenwald enrolled in the Touro Infirmary nursing school in New Orleans. She completed the program, worked for a while in Florida and North Carolina, then went to Johns Hopkins in 1913-1914 for a "post-graduate" course in psychiatric nursing. During this period she met Henrietta Szold, who aroused her interest in Zionism and in a proposal to work in Palestine. With the outbreak of World War I, the plan fell through, and Greenwald went to New York to study at Teachers College, Columbia University while working as a public health nurse in New Jersey. America entered the war in 1917, and in the follow-

Amelia Greenwald, c.1915

Courtesy of her daughter, Liselotte Weil

ing spring Greenwald joined the Army. She served in various psychiatric and base hospitals in France and Germany.

After her discharge from military service, Greenwald was recruited by the National Council of Jewish Women in 1919 to direct its training program for immigrant Jewish women who had settled in farm communities. In 1923, she accepted an appointment under the auspices of the American Joint Distribution Committee to go to Poland where she set up a training school for Jewish nurses at the Jewish Hospital in Warsaw. Her work was internationally recognized, and the Polish government honored her with the presentation of a Gold Cross of Merit. Greenwald maintained contact with her nursing colleagues in the United States who favorably acknowledged her accomplishments in Poland (Roberts, 1931).

After Greenwald left Poland and came back to the United States, she remained active in public health nursing. In the early 1930s, she accepted an invitation to go to Jerusalem where she spent a little over one year working with the Hadassah Nursing School. Soon after Greenwald returned home, she decided to move closer to family members who were living in the South. In 1939, she succeeded in bringing two young distant relatives, a brother and a sister, out of Nazi Germany. Greenwald undertook the care of the young woman, and Greenwald's brother raised the boy. Greenwald continued to live in Eunice, La., until she died at the age of 85 in 1966.

Regina Kaplan (1887-1957)

Regina Kaplan was born in Memphis, Tenn., to Gershon and Adella (Hannah) Traube Kaplan, who were immigrants from Germany. Kaplan had two older siblings and two younger siblings. When she was quite young, the family moved to Denver, Colo., because her mother had developed health problems. Denver was a center for the treatment of tuberculosis (TB)—a major concern in the immigrant Jewish population. It is assumed that her mother had TB. The Jewish Hospital for Consumptives in Denver received wide support from members of the Jewish community.

As a young adult, Kaplan wanted to become a doctor, but this was not within her means. She enrolled at the Mercy Hospital Training School for Nurses in Denver where she finished in 1908 at the top of her class of 12 students. When she entered nursing school, she was barely 17 years old, short of stature, and slightly built. After she completed her program, she became a private duty nurse. With the onset of World War I, she enrolled in the American Red Cross as a preliminary step to joining the Army. She was, however, not accepted for military service, presumably because of her height.

Kaplan continued to do private duty, until she learned of an opening for a nursing superintendent at the Leo N. Levi Hospital in Hot Springs, Ark. The Levi Hospital, formally dedicated in 1916, was established through Bnai Brith as a sanitarium for charity cases. Kaplan became superintendent in 1916, and for the next 35 years her major endeavor was the growth and development of the nursing school. In addition, she was at the center of many community health and welfare projects. She organized and directed a dispensary for outpatients, set up a Red Cross chapter where she taught first aid classes and home nursing to adults, instigated the establishment of a school nursing service and of a public health nursing program, raised funds for the construction of a new nurses home, and so on.

Among her other interests, Kaplan actively participated in professional organizations, including the American Nurses Association, Arkansas and Colorado State Nurses Associations, American College of Hospital Administrators, Arkansas Hospital Association, National Arthritis Research Foundation—just to name a few. During World War II, Kaplan played a key role in community health and welfare programs. In 1944, she was honored by Eleanor Roosevelt at the White House.

Kaplan never married but sought and received the right to care for a newborn infant, who became her adopted daughter. Kaplan also maintained close ties with the Jewish community through the synagogue, Hadassah, and Bnai Brith. She retired from the Levi Hospital in 1951 but served afterward as the director of central supply at another hospital. In September 1957, when it became clear that she was terminally ill with cancer, she moved back to Denver and was admitted to the Jewish hospital, where she died on October 8, 1957. She left a remarkable legacy of dedicated service to nursing and to the entire community (Mayer, 1996; 1997).

Rose Kaplan (1867-1917)

Rose Kaplan was born in Russia in 1867 and came to the United States in 1892. She studied nursing at Mount Sinai Hospital's Nursing School and went on to serve as a nurse in the Spanish-American War. A few years later, she was recruited by Henrietta Szold to organize the Hadassah health service in Palestine. She and her colleague, Rae Landy, accompanied by Mr. and Mrs. Nathan Straus, arrived in Jerusalem in 1913. Kaplan and Landy collaborated in establishing a health center and a visiting nurse service under crude and difficult local conditions. They had made

great strides, but their progress was interrupted by the
World War I. Kaplan went back to the United States a
another Hadassah assignment to work at an Egyptian
Jewish refugees from Palestine.

On her return trip to the Middle East, the ship on wl
was sailing caught fire, and she was sent back to Nev
set out again, and when she reached Alexandria she went to work
caring for patients and distributing needed supplies. Before she
left for Egypt, Kaplan, unfortunately, had undergone surgery for
cancer, and now her health began to fail. She refused to give in
and did not tell her Hadassah employers about her condition. She
continued to work until she died in August 1917. She was buried
in Egypt, but some years later her remains were removed and she
was laid to rest in Jerusalem (Goldstein, 1997).

Rachel (Rae) D. Landy (1885-1952)

A simple, unadorned plaque in the Hadassah Hospital, Jerusalem, has the following inscription in block letters:

NURSES STATION IN MEMORY OF
LT. COLONEL RAE DIANA LANDY
U.S. ARMY NURSE CORPS
PIONEER HADASSAH NURSE IN
PALESTINE
1913-1916
CLEVELAND CHAPTER OF HADASSAH
CLEVELAND, OHIO

Rae D. Landy—Lieutenant Colonel Rae D. Landy at the time
of her death—was born in Lithuania in 1885, one of seven children of Eva (Gross) and Rabbi Jacob Landy. As a small child,
Landy immigrated with her family to Cleveland, Ohio, where
Rabbi Landy had been invited to serve that area as its first *Torah*
scribe (personal communication, Rae Landy's cousin, Edna Goldsmith, February 6, 1992).

In 1904, as a young woman, Landy was among the graduates
in the first class of nursing students of the Jewish Women's Hospital Association (later Mount Sinai Hospital) in Cleveland. After
graduation, Landy did private duty nursing in Cleveland and New
York (Col. Rae D. Landy Dies, 1952) and by 1911, she held an
administrative nursing position at Harlem Hospital in New York
City. This is where she was working when she was recruited by

Henrietta Szold for the Hadassah project in Palestine. Described as a light-hearted, fun-loving woman, Landy sailed for Palestine in 1913 with Rose Kaplan and with Mr. and Mrs. Nathan Straus (Levin, 1997). In Jerusalem, Landy and Kaplan were successful in setting up a system of preventive health care and in laying the foundation for the vast network of services provided by Hadassah in Israel today. The nurses stayed until the program was suspended after the outbreak of World War I.

Rae Landy returned home, where, in 1918, she enlisted in the military and served overseas with the American Expeditionary Force in World War I. Landy continued to serve her country into World War II, retiring in 1944 as a lieutenant colonel, the second highest rank in the Army Nurse Corps at that time. After retirement, she worked with the American Red Cross and recruited nurses for Mount Sinai Hospital until her death in March 1952, after which she was laid to rest in Arlington National Cemetery (Benson, 1990; Johnson, 1997).

Hilda Salomon (1895-1983)

As a pioneer nurse-anesthetist, Hilda Salomon was a highly respected and widely recognized leader who contributed significantly to the advancement of her field of nursing practice. Born in Massachusetts in 1895 to Sadie (Wolfe) and Abraham Harris, Hilda Salomon experienced personal tragedy early in life. One of four children, she was orphaned by the age of 10. She grew up in Lynn, Mass., where she and her siblings were raised by their grandmother. In 1916, she was married to Leo Salomon, who died in a work-related accident just a few months later. It was after this event that Hilda Salomon entered nursing school at the Union Hospital in Lynn. In her own words, "As far back as I can remember, my greatest ambition was to serve people: the sick, the poor, and the underprivileged" (Salomon, 1981, p. 14).

Salomon completed nursing school in 1920, and at the invitation of one of her cousins, she came to Philadelphia, where she worked for a while at a small hospital. Soon afterward, she decided to enter the training program for nurse-anesthetists at Lankenau Hospital School of Anesthesia in Philadelphia, which she completed in 1923 (personal communication with cousin of Hilda Salomon, January 26, 1996). She accepted a position as a nurse-anesthetist at the Jewish Hospital in Philadelphia, where she was

Hilda Salomon

Courtesy of the American Association of Nurse Anesthetists Archives Library

appointed in 1924 as chief of the Department of Anesthesia. Salomon placed great emphasis on education and planned and organized regular meetings for her colleagues to hear key speakers and to learn about new developments in anesthesia. In 1929, Salomon launched the Jewish Hospital School of Anesthesia, which graduated 218 nurse-anesthetists during the 18 years it was in operation.

Along with a group of her colleagues, Salomon participated in the establishment of the National Association of Nurse Anesthetists in 1931, which in 1939 became known as the American Association of Nurse Anesthetists (AANA). Salomon was president of the organization from 1935-1937. She also was instrumental in organizing the Pennsylvania Association of Nurse Anesthetists in which she held the office of president. As a leader in her professional organization, Salomon was a strong advocate of human rights, and her ideas were considered radical by many of her peers (AANA Pioneer Hilda Salomon Dies, 1984). In her own words, "I recall one great problem which faced the Association [AANA] during the early years; the admission of black and male nurse anesthetists, properly trained, into our Association. Many harsh words were exchanged. It wasn't until 1944-47 that my original idea was accepted" (Salomon, 1981). One source indicates that her proposal was bitterly attacked by the board members and that part of the opposition leveled at Salomon at that time stemmed from the fact that she was Jewish (Benson, 2000).

In 1948, Salomon resigned as Chief Anesthetist at the Philadelphia Jewish Hospital; after that, she continued to work and to remain professionally active. Colleagues and former students recall her as a person of great professional dignity and integrity who radiated personal warmth and commanded everyone's respect. Toward the end of her life, she went to live with a cousin in Florida, where she died at the age of 88 in 1983.

Mathilda Scheuer (1890-1974)

A leader in public health nursing, Mathilda Scheuer was devoted to creating a better society and to strengthening the nursing profession. What little is known about her early life comes from an interview for a press release upon her re-election as 18th president of the American Nurses' Association in 1960. Scheuer was born in Berryville, Clarke County, Va., to "Lizzie" and Louis Scheuer, the fourth oldest of seven children. Her father emigrated at the age of 14 from Frankfurt, Germany, and settled in the Shenandoah Valley. As far back as she could remember, Scheuer had always wanted to be a nurse and attributed this goal to her father, who taught his children that "you must never turn anybody down who needs help." Following her graduation in 1910 from the Mercy Hospital School of Nursing in Baltimore, she went into private duty nursing and took an active role in professional nursing organizations.

After the United States entered World War I, Scheuer tried to enlist for overseas duty, but she was turned down. An opportunity came along for her to go into public health nursing when she joined the staff of the Philadelphia Visiting Nurse Society. In 1920, she enrolled in the public health nursing program at the University of Pennsylvania, which she later completed, and she went on for additional training at Teachers College, Columbia Univer-

Mathilda Scheuer

Courtesy of Charlotte and Louis Rosenthal, niece and nephew of Mathilda Scheuer

sity. It was in Philadelphia through the Visiting Nurse Society that Scheuer found the broader service that she had been seeking. On public transportation and on foot, she made the rounds to serve those who needed her help. She advanced from assistant supervisor to supervisor and then from assistant education director to education director. She became the assistant general director and then acting director of the agency, a position she held at the time of her retirement in 1956.

Throughout her long career, Scheuer sought ways to serve others and to stand up for the weak and dispossessed. She worked tirelessly to safeguard the rights of nurses and to strengthen the position of the American Nurses' Association. She was not afraid to call for change, and she did not hesitate to promote sound new ideas even if they did not conform to the accepted views of her peers. Born and raised in the South, she was brought up in a liberal tradition and held passionate convictions as an advocate of civil rights and human rights. She demanded these rights for African American nurses, and as president of the American Nurses' Association (1958-1962) she led the campaign to end racial discrimination in the organization. Although people did not always agree with her, no one ever questioned Scheuer's integrity and intellectual honesty. She remained professionally active even after her retirement from the Visiting Nurse Society. Scheuer died in 1974, at the age of 84 (Benson, 1988).

Rosa Zimmern Van Vort (1876-1944)

Rosa Zimmern Van Vort was a nursing leader in Virginia in the early 20th century. She was born in Richmond in 1876, the daughter of Isaac and Hettie (Zimmern) Van Vort. At the age of 21, she became a nursing student at the Old Dominion Hospital Training School for Nurses of the Medical College of Virginia. After graduation, she went on for further training in Philadelphia and then on to Teachers College, Columbia University in New York.

Van Vort returned to Richmond, where, in 1904, she became superintendent of nurses and head of the training school in the Medical College of Virginia's new teaching facility, the Memorial Hospital. In 1913, she organized and directed the training school at the newly established Stuart Circle Hospital in Richmond, where she stayed until 1924. After that she served briefly as superintendent at St. Elizabeth Hospital in Richmond and then spent

Rosa Zimmern Van Vort

Special Collections and Archives, Tompkins McCaw Library, Virginia Commonwealth University

one year in Knoxville, Tenn., where she organized the nursing school at the General Hospital. She returned to Virginia where she retired.

Throughout her career, Van Vort played an active role in professional nursing organizations and served four terms as President of the Virginia State League of Nursing, which was organized in 1918. She strived to improve the quality of training and to reduce work hours for nursing students. During World War I, Van Vort was active in the recruitment and enrollment of nurses through state and city councils of defense and the Red Cross. For this, she received a special award in 1922. In later years, she suffered ill health, and in February 1944, she died at home (Koste, 1997).

Summary

This chapter has presented brief biographical sketches of several Jewish women who added luster to the nursing profession in the first half of the 20th century. Nearly all of these women or their parents came from Central or Eastern Europe from that generation of Jewish immigrants who, in seeking a better life for themselves and for their children in the United States, enriched the social, scientific, and cultural fabric of their new country.

Most of these women were steeped in a liberal tradition and were motivated by high ideals. There was great variation in the Jewish background of each of them. Some were from strongly religious, observant Jewish homes. Others were from families who were not religious, but were culturally bound to Jewish tradition. Some came from a well-integrated, mainstream American background. All of them, however, shared a common identity through their Jewish heritage. The list could go on to include many others who have not as yet been identified as being Jewish. But, perhaps, the examples cited in this chapter illustrate, at least as a beginning, that nursing is and was and always will be for a Jewish girl! (*and* for a Jewish boy, too).

As the 20th century unfolded and drew to a close, indeed, many Jewish women entered nursing. In the next part of this book, we see how some of these women fared within the ranks of the profession. Part Two (Chapters 6 through 10) shows the presence of Jewish women in contemporary nursing. Chapter 6 describes the search for Jewish nurses through an informal survey launched in 1990 by this author. Chapters 7-9 present the experiences described by Jewish nurses who responded to the survey, and Chapter 10 features the movement by Jewish nurses to network through the newly established Nurses Councils of Hadassah, the Women's Zionist Organization of America.

References

AANA Pioneer Hilda Salomon Dies. (1984, January). *AANA News Bulletin.* Park Ridge, IL: American Association of Nurse Anesthetists.

Baer, E. (1991, February 23). The feminist disdain for nursing. *New York Times.*

Benson, E. R. (1987). Josephine Goldmark (1877-1950): A biographic sketch. *Public Health Nursing, 4* (1), 48-51.

Benson, E. R. (1988). Mathilda Scheuer (1890-1974): A biographical sketch. *The Pennsylvania Nurse, 43* (5), 6, 10.

Benson, E. R. (1990). Hadassah and the nursing connection: Early days. *Bulletin of the American Association for the History of Nursing 26,* 4-6.

Benson, E. R. (2000). Hilda Salomon. In V. L. Bullough & L. Sentz (Eds.), *American nursing – A biographical dictionary. Vol. 3.* New York: Springer.

Brody, S. (1996). Margaret Arnstein: Nursing educator and public health nurse. *Jewish heroes and heroines in America, 1900 to World War II:* A Judaica Collection. Florida Atlantic University Libraries. (*http://www.fau.edu*)

Bullough, V. L., Church, O. M., & Stein, A. P. (1988). *American nursing: A biographical dictionary.* New York: Garland Publishing.

Col. Rae D. Landy Dies, Headed Nurses at Crile. (1952, March 6). Obituary in *Cleveland Press.*

Daniels, D. G. (1989). *Always a sister: The feminism of Lillian D. Wald.* New York: The Feminist Press.

Fondiller, S. (1988). Margaret Gene Arnstein, 1904-1972. In V. L. Bullough, O. M. Church, & A. P. Stein, *American nursing: A biographical dictionary* (pp. 8-12). New York: Garland Publishing.

Goldstein, E. L. (1997). Kaplan, Rose (1867-1917). In P. E. Hyman & D. D. Moore, *Jewish women in America: A historical encyclopedia.* New York: Routledge.

Hayton-Keeva, S. (Ed.). (1987). Esther Blanc in *Valiant women in war and exile: Thirty-eight true stories.* San Francisco: City Lights Books.

James, J. W. (1984). Writing and re-writing nursing history: A review essay. *Bulletin of the History of Medicine, 58,* 568-584.

James, E. T. (Ed.). (1971). *Notable American women, 1607-1950. Vol. II.* Cambridge, MA: Belknap Press of Harvard University.

Johnson, B. D. (1997). Rae D. Landy (1885-1952). In P. E. Hyman & D. D. Moore, *Jewish women in America: A historical encyclopedia.* New York: Routledge.

Koste, J. (1997). Rosa Zimmern Van Vort (1876-1944). In P. E. Hyman & D. D. Moore, *Jewish women in America: A historical encyclopedia.* New York: Routledge.

Levin, M. (1997). *It takes a dream: The story of Hadassah.* New York: Geffen Books.

Mayer, S. L. (1994). Amelia Greenwald: Pioneer in international public health nursing. *Nursing and Health Care,* 15(2), 74-78.

Mayer, S. L. A. (1996). *The Jewish experience in nursing in America: 1881 to 1955.* Ann Arbor, MI: University Microfilms International (Doctoral Dissertation).

Mayer, S. L. (1997). Kaplan, Regina (1887-1957). In P. E. Hyman & D. D. Moore, *Jewish women in America: A historical encyclopedia.* New York: Routledge.

Roberts, M. (1931). Analysis of fundamental resemblances and differences in representative systems of nursing education. *International aspects of nursing education, from lectures presented February 12 to April 23, 1931.* Nursing Education Department of Teachers College, Columbia University: Bureau of Publications.

Roberts, M. M. (1954). *American nursing: History and interpretation.* New York: Macmillan.

Salomon, H. (1981). Hilda Salomon . . . A half century of memories: A 50 year Retrospective. *American Association of Nurse Anesthetists 1931-1981.* Park Ridge, IL: American Association of Nurse Anesthetists (AANA).

Sokoloff, L. (1994). Amelia Greenwald (1881-1966): Pioneer American-Jewish nurse. *Korot, 10,* 92-101.

$\mathcal{P}$art II

The Jewish Presence in Contemporary Nursing

6

✡ "Jewish Nurses? There Aren't Any!"
or How And Why The Search Began

Introduction

"Jewish nurses? There aren't any, are there?" "Oh, I didn't think Jewish women went into nursing." "Jewish women don't want to be nurses, they don't want to get their hands dirty." Expressions such as these have a ring of familiarity to many Jewish nurses who have chosen to enter a profession that has been linked primarily with the tradition of Christianity. As a young woman growing up in a Jewish family and entering nursing in the first half of the 20th century, I was one of those nurses. Finally, after hearing these and other bizarre and insulting myths and half-truths, I decided that an issue had emerged that should be addressed.

In the early 1980s, I approached some of my colleagues informally with the idea of exploring the presence of Jewish women in nursing. Their reactions reflected a lot of skepticism and were very dispiriting. The non-Jewish colleagues believed the widespread notion that "there are no Jewish nurses," and the Jewish nurses did not see any special relevance to this idea. Jewish nurses apparently preferred to maintain a low profile and to minimize their visibility within the larger nursing community. They also seemed slow in reacting to the cultural, societal, and political realities of multiculturalism in late 20th century America.

In this respect, Jewish nurses were probably following the lead of the larger Jewish community, which, from the earliest days of their immigration into this country, accepted the "melting pot" ideal. Within the Jewish community, a focus on ethnicity was generally subordinated to the goal of entering mainstream society as fully participating members. The ideal of equal opportunity captivated the psyche of most immigrant Jews. The fondest dreams of immigrant Jewish parents were realized when they watched their children set forth each day to attend public school with all of the other children—*gleich wie alle*, "just like everyone else," as they would say in Yiddish, nodding with satisfaction. They were free from the patterns of the "old country," where they had been confronted by quotas or the need to bribe public officials when they wanted to send their children to school. From the moment they stepped onto American soil as immigrants, American Jews welcomed opportunities for equal participation and acceptance in an open world.

Within the framework of contemporary society, a new dimension exists whereby Jewish concerns tend to be excluded when multicultural issues are treated. In the Jewish community, the response to this exclusion has been varied. For example, the well-known novelist and scholar, Chaim Potok, in a public address, characterized this exclusion as a natural and acceptable outcome of "successful" Jewish integration into the larger society (Leiter, 1992). Others, however, believe that, in reality, the Jewish community is still a minority in America and, as such, confronts barriers just as other minorities do. Similarly, it may be said that Jewish nurses are a minority within the nursing community and, only recently, have some of them begun to voice concerns in the same way as other minorities have done.

Over the years, Jewish nurses as a group did not emulate other nursing groups who had formed national networks or coalitions based on ethnic or other special identities, such as the National Black Nurses Association, National Hispanic Nurses Association, National Organization of Philippine Nurses in the United States, Nurses Christian Fellowship, and so on. However, under the influence of a growing societal preoccupation with ethnic identity, Jewish nurses began in 1990 to network through the National Nurses Councils within the framework of Hadassah, the Women's Zionist Organization of America. When the call went out through local chapters of the organization, Jewish nurses from towns and cities across the nation expressed great interest in establishing their own councils. Within 3 years, over 25 local councils were formed in 18 states.

These results were rather stirring in view of the prevailing notion that there are so few Jewish nurses within the ranks of the nursing profession and the fact that Jewish nurses had been opting for a low profile. It is impossible to say with any accuracy just how many Jewish nurses there are. The most recent comprehensive survey of the Jewish population in the United States indicated that 10% of American Jews were employed in medical and health fields, but no classification by specific occupation was done (Benson, 1994). Nor is there any identifying information in the statistical tabulation of the Registered Nurse population. For example, the U.S. Department of Health and Human Services Survey of the Registered Nurse Population (RNP Survey) (Moses, 1992) officially recognizes four racial/ethnic minority backgrounds: Black (non-Hispanic), Asian/Pacific Islanders, Hispanic, and American Indian/Alaskan Native.

The RNP Survey does not tabulate Jewish nurses as an ethnically identifiable group. Nor would Jewish nurses particularly welcome such a practice. Jews, in general, have traditionally advocated policies that would eliminate ethnic labeling. As a community they have been understandably wary of official governmental classification and institutionalization of ethnic identity. Time and again in various countries throughout history, such practices have had dire consequences for the Jewish people.

With the accumulation of myths and stereotypes about Jewish women and their disinclination to go into nursing, it was time for a response, particularly in view of mounting public emphasis on ethnic identity. In addition, nursing has created a more congenial climate, as it has begun to recognize the contributions of diverse groups to the development of the profession. For me, the question remained, "What is the extent of the presence of Jewish women in nursing?" I acted on an earlier impulse and undertook a search in 1990 for Jewish nurses in the United States.

The Initial Response

The search began modestly. I made personal contact with Jewish nurse colleagues and reached out on a one-to-one basis to nurses who had identified themselves as being Jewish. In addition, I placed a notice about seeking data on Jewish women in nursing in various bulletins and newsletters that would reach Jewish nurses. Encouraged by the response, I tried for wider dissemination by sending my inquiry to Jewish newspapers in other parts of the country. I had no way of ascertaining how many of these publications actually printed my request, and because of the general perception that "there are no Jewish nurses," I did not expect to receive many replies. Hence, it was a pleasant surprise to receive over 200 responses from Georgia, Maryland, Massachusetts, Nebraska, New York, Pennsylvania, Tennessee, Texas, Wisconsin, and other parts of the country.

The letters were very enthusiastic:

"I was interested to read of your request in our Jewish press." "I'm just thrilled that someone has finally taken an interest in this subject." "I want to commend you on your efforts and wish you the best of luck." "How wonderful that you are researching this issue! Please feel free to contact me." "It was with great pleasure that I read your letter in The Jewish Times; I cannot count the number of times I have been told that I am a fine example of Christian nursing. It is always meant as a compliment, but it drives me to distraction." "There is entirely too much emphasis on the Christianity of nursing and I applaud your study." "I am a Jewish woman in nursing. I encounter people on a daily basis [who] cannot believe that I could possibly be a nurse and Jewish as well. I cannot imagine choosing another profession over nursing." "What a noble effort! More power to you." "I look forward to hearing more about your study." "I'm an RN from Brooklyn Jewish Hospital, a graduate of 1944. I've loved every minute of my nursing days. . . . How can I help you?"

These were typical comments from nurses who responded to the letters of inquiry that had appeared in various newspapers and bulletins. There were scores of similarly positive responses. How very different were these reactions from those elicited when the idea of conducting a survey on a smaller scale had been suggested a decade earlier. Clearly, something had changed in the intervening years, which had given rise to an increased awareness and appreciation of one's Jewish identity. Jewish nurses were beginning to seek recognition. The respondents were overwhelmingly positive concerning the idea of identifying and describing the Jewish presence in nursing.

Other highlights were noted in the initial responses. For example, the interest of family and friends, and their degree of participation, was striking. Often a cousin, daughter, son, niece, father, mother, or friend had notified respondents about the study. Examples of some of the responses are as follows:

"A friend of mine … showed me your letter to the editor. Please let me know if I could be of help." "My mother who will soon be 80 years old was a registered nurse. She was raised in an Orthodox Jewish home; she might be a good candidate for your study." "My daughter is a nurse practitioner . . . I think she would wish to participate." "Both my mother and I are RNs; we are both very proud of our profession and would enjoy being part of your study."

In one instance, a woman wrote to say that her brother was a nurse. Several non-nurses sent lists of names of Jewish nurse friends who they thought would be interested. One woman wrote to share information about her deceased aunts whom she considered to be pioneer nurses in the Jewish community in early 20th century America. One person sent an item from his Pennsylvania State University alumni bulletin (n.d.) about a nurse with a "Jewish-sounding surname" who had pioneered in nursing education at Northern Illinois University and Idaho State University. One man replied rather wistfully saying that he wished he could find a nice Jewish nurse who would want to marry him!

The respondents represented a variety of specialties—hospital staff nurses, public health nurses, school nurses, home health care nurses, nursing educators and administrators, hospice nurses, former deans, nurse practitioners, ambulatory care nurses, entrepreneurs, and two nurses who had gone into politics and served with distinction in their state legislature for many years. Over one-half of the respondents followed up their initial response with a more detailed personalized and informal narrative based on a questionnaire for compiling an oral history (Donahue, 1982).

The material was reviewed and summarized. Information about the general population of nurses was gathered from the study, The Registered Nurse Population 1992, in order to provide a frame of reference that might be helpful with regard to the group of Jewish nurses who responded. The respondents came from a variety of Jewish backgrounds, some very strongly connected to Judaism, others not. Nearly four-fifths were born and lived in large metropolitan areas or their suburbs, and one-fifth were born and lived in small towns. These figures are similar to the population of nurses in general (Moses, 1992). Ages reported ranged from 22 to 102; the average age was 53.8 years for the study and for the general nursing population it was 43.1 years (Moses, 1992). Concerning the survey group being somewhat older than was the general nursing population, it should be noted that the initial letter of inquiry indicated that I was especially interested in hearing from Jewish nurses who entered nursing school up to and including the period of World War II.

In responding to a question about where they had studied nursing, more than one-half of the respondents indicated that they had completed programs in schools associated with Jewish hospitals. Some pointed out that they chose a Jewish hospital school of nursing at their parents' urging or because they themselves wanted a connection with a Jewish institution; others explained that they had been denied admission to non-Jewish schools where it was made clear that they were not welcome because of their Jewish background. Of those who listed their educational credentials, the highest level of education reported was 44% diploma or associate degree, 29% bachelor's, 19.1% master's, and 7.4% doctoral degree. For the general nursing population, the highest level of education was 61% diploma or associate degree, 30% bachelor's, 7.5% master's, and 0.5% doctoral degree (Moses, 1992).

Concerning employment, of those who included information, 58% were working in responsible positions in roles as educators, administrators, researchers, public health nurses, school nurses, private entrepreneurs, nurse practitioners, clinical specialists, and so on; 14% were working at staff level in various settings, such as hospitals, long-term care, and so on; 4% were either in graduate school or were looking for new employment; 24% were retired. Of those who provided information about their continuity in nursing practice, 8% indicated that they had "dropped out"; for the general population of nurses, the rate was 12% (Moses, 1992); 11% had "stopped out" of nursing for a few years, usually when their children were small and then returned.

These were some of the characteristics of Jewish nurses as indicated by the women who sent in the information about themselves. It is interesting to note some of the similarities between them and the general population of nurses (place of residence and baccalaureate education level), as well as some of the differences (average age, advanced education level, and rate of drop out).

We do not know with any degree of certainty the total number of Jewish nurses in this country. To be proportionally represented within the general population of nurses, which is about 2.2 million, there would have to be about 40,000-45,000 Jewish nurses. According to the Hadassah National Center of Nurses Councils, there are probably no more than 16,000 Jewish nurses, and this is a high estimate. Thus, we realize that, although Jewish nurses, numerically, are proportionally underrepresented in the general population of nurses, ample evidence exists to challenge the notion about the lack of a Jewish presence in nursing. "Jewish nurses? There aren't any!" is a myth that should be laid to rest. The time has come to debunk this and other myths and stereotypes about Jewish nurses.

Summary

In recent years, under the influence of society's increased emphasis on ethnic identity and ethnic diversity, there is a growing recognition within the nursing profession that it is important to acknowledge and to respect the contributions of diverse ethnic and racial groups. Concomitantly, Jewish nurses, more so now than in the past, have shown an interest in exploring their heritage and in acknowledging their presence in the larger nursing community. For example, they responded enthusiastically to a request for participation in a survey, whereas 10 years earlier the mere suggestion of such a survey was greeted with derision. And, finally, Jewish nurses have sought networking opportunities through nurses councils established by Hadassah. Yes, there are Jewish nurses; and, yes, they do get their hands dirty; and, yes, they want their presence known.

References

Benson, E. R. (1994). Jewish nurses: A multicultural perspective. *Journal of the New York State Nurses Association, 25*(2), 8-10.

Donahue, E. M. (1982). Preserving history through oral history reflections. *Journal of Gerontological Nursing, 8*(5), 274.

Leiter, R. (1992). *The Jewish exponent:* America is still struggling with its cultural pluralism. Philadelphia: Jewish Federation of Greater Philadelphia.

Moses, E. B. (1992). *The registered nurse population 1992. National sample survey of registered nurses, March 1992.* Washington, DC: U.S. Dept. of Health and Human Services, Health Resources and Services Administration, Division of Nursing. Pennsylvania State University Alumni Bulletin, (n.d.).

7

How Did Our Parents and Families *Really* Feel About It? or "Jewish Girls Don't Do That!" Versus "My Daughter, The Nurse!"

One of the stereotypes about Jewish women in nursing arises from the perception that Jewish parents and other family members react negatively to nursing as a desirable career choice. This is a persistent and troublesome myth that has been targeted at Jewish people. Why does it persist? As with most myths and legends, it probably has some basis in fact. But if one considers how non-Jewish parents and other family members react, one would likely find evidence to suggest that even non-Jews sometimes object when one of their young women wants to become a nurse.

For example, I interviewed an elderly, retired, non-Jewish nurse for a historical study of the public health nursing agency that she had directed in the 1960s. She recalled how her father had been violently opposed to her choice when she announced that she wanted to enter nursing school in 1931. "He was an old country Dutchman, and he roared, 'No daughter of mine . . . !'"

And yet, this comment is made so often about Jewish families that it became an issue for this survey about Jewish women in nursing. The women who responded were asked to give special attention to the question, "How did your family or friends feel about your wanting to become a nurse? Did any of them try to dissuade you or persuade you to do something else? Why?" Almost 60% of the respondents reported that their families or friends reacted positively to their decision to enter nursing. The remaining 40% reported that the reactions of their parents or other members of their family were neutral or mixed, or, in some cases, decidedly negative, such as "Ugh, Jewish girls don't do that." However, after their daughters had completed their programs, many of the parents who had expressed negative feelings were bursting with pride at "My daughter, the nurse." To further neutralize this particular myth, I point out that many sets of mother-daughter, sister-sister, aunt-niece, and cousin relatives were among the respondents. Even some three-generational sets of nurses responded. In all, fewer than 10% of the narratives reflected strongly negative views on the part of family members or friends.

A description of the reactions and views of parents, other family members, or friends as described by respondents is presented here. In the spirit of preserving anonymity and maintaining confidentiality, pseudonyms have been assigned. The first group of statements includes those of Jewish women who experienced positive reactions from all or most of their loved ones.

"My Family Thought it Was Wonderful!"

Reactions of family members and friends in this group were essentially positive and even enthusiastic, reflecting a wholesome attitude toward nursing. The responses of the nurses are divided into several categories that indicate a variety of incentives and motives for why they chose nursing as a career. The first category of this group reflects a view of nursing as a highly respected, noble, honorable profession. Parents were described as being proud of their daughters for having a career and for having chosen nursing.

Rose R., age 73, described how she grew up in a poverty-stricken neighborhood where hers was the only Jewish family.

> When I was a little girl I used to go around with
> my mother who was considered to be the "neigh-
> borhood nurse". . . the healer. From her came my
> desire to be a nurse. I was the first one [in my
> family] to go into nursing.

Rose's family thought it was wonderful and was very proud of her. She had their full support in her decision.

Arline A. wrote, "I decided to become a nurse as soon as I graduated from high school." Arline completed nursing school in 1962. Her decision to go into nursing was influenced by her aunt, a nurse who was strongly dedicated to her profession. "My family encouraged my entering nursing because it is a great profession and because they all admired my aunt so much."

Abby A., who studied at a Jewish hospital school of nursing, wrote:

> At age 13 [in the early 1940s] I viewed a film in
> school on visiting nurses at work. That did it! I
> had no idea [about what nursing would be like],
> just that it was compelling and *mitzva-dik* [i.e.,
> the proper thing for a Jewish person to do]. My
> mother, in particular, took it for granted that I
> would enter the profession, since it was my wish.

Bessie B. completed nursing school in 1931 and worked in nursing until she was 70. She was the daughter of immigrants who were "not opposed to" her decision to enter nursing. However, they would not let her enter until they had looked into the situation, and because she had chosen a Jewish hospital nursing school, it was acceptable to them. They were very proud of their daughter for having a career.

Emily E., now in her mid-30s, wrote that she was the "first in my family to take up nursing; my parents were Holocaust survivors and were very proud of me and of whatever I wanted to do."

Eileen E., who completed her BSN in 1979, had this to say:

> I'm not sure when I finally decided to be a nurse.
> It was probably in 10th or 11th grade when I final-
> ized my decision. My parents were extremely
> supportive, as they have always been, and felt
> that I was entering a very noble profession. I am
> the first and only nurse in our family and I know
> they are very proud. While I was in college, my
> mother would always go into great detail with
> friends and relatives as to what I was learning
> because she was amazed and impressed at what
> nurses really have to know. . . . A couple of
> elderly aunts thought that a nice "perk" would be
> meeting all those "nice, young doctors," but they,
> too, are supportive and proud.

Cynthia C., a young woman in her early 30s, recalled that for as long as she could remember, she had wanted to be a nurse. She would accompany her father, who was a physician, when he made hospital rounds. She would wait for him in the nurses station, where they would make a big fuss over her. "I would sit there and color with their red pens." Her father tried to push her toward medicine, and she finally said to him, "I love you but I want to be a nurse and I don't want to be a doctor." Her family supported her in her decision and eventually came to understand her commitment to nursing and to respect her decision. Her grandmother had a gift of caring and understanding illness. Her paternal grandfather was very proud of her, and when she came to visit him at his retirement home, he would introduce her by saying, "This is my granddaughter, the nurse."

Fern F., who just turned 41, recalled, "I don't remember ever not wanting to be a nurse. Helping people was my image [of nursing]." She believed that she was drawn to nursing because her mother was a nurse. Everyone in her family and in her future husband's family were supportive and still are.

An interesting point is that Rose, Emily, and Eileen were the first in their families to enter nursing. On the other hand, Arline's aunt was a nurse who influenced her, and Fern was drawn to nursing because her mother was a nurse. The next set of narratives shows a similar pattern of women who came from families in which others had preceded them in nursing and in which the profession was highly regarded.

Evelyn E. wrote, "I wanted to be a nurse ever since I can remember. My mother was a nurse. My father and my family had a very high regard for her work. My family was all for it."

Bertha B. was a 76-year-old nurse from a Conservative Jewish background. She explained:

> When I was 14 years old, I decided that I wanted to be a nurse. The image at that time was one of respect. My mother influenced my decision to become a nurse since she was a registered nurse from the first class of nurses to be registered as RNs in the Commonwealth of Pennsylvania.

Her father was a veterinarian. Her parents and all of her family supported her decision.

Cindy C., a young woman who was graduated from a school of practical nursing in 1974, went back to her teen years to trace her decision to pursue nursing. In high school she belonged to a future nurses club. "Nurses were viewed as very special people . . . kind, caring, and respected." Her aunt was a registered nurse; her family and friends were very proud of her decision to become a nurse.

Brenda B., who is in her early forties, explained that she decided on nursing as a career when she was in junior high school. Her aunt was a nurse whose role in World War II seemed very interesting. "My decision for nursing was an accepted one. Nursing in my family was already established. There were RNs, LPNs, and Red Cross workers. The men were doctors, of course!"

Jill J., now in her mid-40s, entered nursing as a second career about 7 years ago.

> My grandmother—a pioneer in her day—was a registered nurse, graduating in 1909 from the Connecticut Training School for Nurses, now a part of Yale University. My older sister is also a registered nurse. . . . There you have it—three Jewish nurses in the same family.

Leslie L. completed nursing school in 1972. Her mother and several of her aunts were nurses. Her mother had completed her program in the early 1940s and served in the military in World War II. "I always remember wanting to be a nurse. I was a candy striper; other Jewish girls did not do candy striping." Her decision was partly influenced by her mother's connection to nursing. She had the complete support of her family; her decision to enter nursing was "perfectly fine with them."

Other nurses cited the supportive role of their families, and, at the same time, they identified motives related to economic security as reasons for entering nursing. "Nursing was a practical thing to do." Some were pushed into selecting a nursing career because it offered an opportunity to make a living and be independent. Consider, for example, the narratives of the sisters, Bernice and Clara (below), who referred to bad economic times during the Great Depression. Others spoke of the appeal to patriotism during World War II.

Emma E. reported that she completed nursing school in 1952.

> I was a senior in high school when I decided to become a nurse. It was considered an honorable profession. My mother was concerned that I find a way "to make a living." My choice was supported and encouraged by my family and friends.

Karla K. was in 12th grade when she decided that she wanted to be a nurse because it was a practical thing to do. Her family was very supportive and she entered a diploma program in 1974.

Bernice B. reported that her extended family included several nurses and several generations of nurses. Her parents died in the 1920s, when she was very young. She and her siblings were being raised by her aunt and uncle. Her oldest sister (Clara) entered nursing school at age 17. Her aunt had a daughter, Hortense, whom Bernice admired as a role model. Hortense wanted to be a nurse, and the family decided that Bernice should go into nursing with her. Bernice did not go willingly because she had wanted to be a lawyer. As it turned out, Bernice loved it from the first moment. "The happiest I've ever been in my life, for the first time I had my own bed." Hortense, on the other hand, hated it and wanted to leave from the first moment. Several other cousins attended the same nursing school at various periods, and their surname became very well known among the alumnae members.

Clara C. (Bernice's sister) wrote the following:

> Those were bad economic times. I was very young, 17 years old. They had to pull a few strings to get me [into nursing school] because I was under age. . . . I got in even though I hadn't finished high school. [The family was supportive]; in fact, it was more their decision than mine. I had not even thought about training school, but I was glad to get in. It was where I belonged.

Beth B. reported completing her basic diploma program at a non-Jewish hospital school. She went on to earn advanced degrees, including a doctoral degree from a prestigious university. Beth had chosen nursing, as she said, by the process of elimination. It was during the Depression when her parents died, and she went to work as a secretary. However, she left her job in order to stay at home and provide stability for her three siblings and herself. When they all married, she realized that she needed to "do something," and she recalled how nice the nurses had been to her mother during her hospitalization. She realized that with a career in nursing she would always have a job and a place to live, and it seemed "like a natural thing for me to do." It was her decision without any outside influence from family members.

Adena A. explained that her decision to enter nursing at the age of 17 was largely influenced by the fact that World War II was in progress. Her family was very supportive. Similarly, Charlotte C. was 18 years old, and our country was in World War II in Europe and the

Far East. When she decided to enter nursing school, her family went along with her decision. She was the only one in her family who ever became a nurse, and they were all very proud of her.

Several respondents traced their interest in nursing back to their childhoods, some as early as 4 or 5 years of age, citing their desire to help people. Overall, their families were supportive. One respondent (Janet J.) pointed out that her family's negative view of nursing was transformed by her innate skill as a 12-year-old in helping to care for her grandmother!

Catherine C., now in her mid-50s, claimed that when she was still a child, she knew that she wanted to become a nurse to do something to help people. She lived in a small town near a major hospital and was impressed by seeing the nurses in their uniforms. An older cousin, who had gone into nursing, loved her work and encouraged her to become a nurse. Catherine, in turn, served as a role model for another cousin, Annette, who entered nursing with her. The reactions of family and friends were decidedly positive.

Barbara B., now in her 50s, wrote that: "As far back as I can remember, I have always wanted to be a nurse, probably since I was 4 or 5 years old." In high school, she was active in the nursing club and said, "My image of nursing was very positive, and several of my friends in high school also went to nursing school." Her mother was a nurse (see Bella B.); her father was a social worker. Barbara received a scholarship from a Jewish women's organization and entered a school of nursing at a Jewish-affiliated hospital. She went on to have an interesting and satisfying career as well as a productive and rewarding family life.

Lorraine L. recalled that from a very early age she wanted to be a nurse and to help people. She was the first in her family to go into nursing. "My family did not object; there was no money to do anything else," she said. And she had her mother's support.

Janet J., a graduate of an associate degree nursing program, wrote the following:

> For as long as I can remember, I had always wanted to become a nurse. My parents had the notion that "Jewish girls don't become nurses." It wasn't until my Bubbie got sick and lived with us that my mother realized I had some talent to be a nurse—I was 12 years old! So in 1976 I graduated in the first Associate Degree in Nursing (ADN) class at [my] university.

Mona M. studied nursing in the early 1960s. She said she always wanted to be a nurse. Her father was a physician, whom she used to help in his office. Mona had the impression that most Jewish women went into teaching rather than into nursing. She made the decision on her own without being influenced by anyone. Because her family and friends thought it was a good idea, no one tried to dissuade her.

Adele A. wrote the following:

> From the time I was a small child I wanted to be a nurse. Back then one had to be a nurse to be an airline stewardess, and that was what I wanted to be. My parents encouraged me in whatever I wanted to do, as long as I had an education or trade after high school.

Adele completed nursing school then entered military service during WW II.

Another segment of respondents pointed out that they had first considered nursing but then changed their minds. Later some of them entered nursing as a second career, or as a second choice, or even "by default." They cited practical reasons for choosing nursing, such as a need to develop a marketable skill, have a stable career, or achieve independence.

Sandra S., now in her mid-40s, said that as a little girl, she had wanted to be a nurse. Her interests changed and she went to college where she earned a degree in biology. It was after she was married and had two children that she began to think about nursing; she had been working as a volunteer with the LaLeche League where she was doing health teaching. Her decision to go into nursing was "purely practical—nursing was a marketable skill, and that was what I needed." Members of her family were enthusiastic about her decision—her husband and mother were very supportive.

Harriet H., age 27, chose nursing as a second career. She wanted a career that offered stability and provided an opportunity to earn a living. It was her own decision, and no one tried to change her mind. Her husband and parents supported her in this decision.

Elizabeth E. reported in her mid-40s that she began a career in nursing in her late 20s after she had already earned another baccalaureate degree and was looking for a career change. She chose a fine collegiate program with a strong academic base. She experienced no family preferences for or against her decision.

Gail G. reported in her early 20s that she chose nursing almost by default—in completing an application for college, she had to fill in her major. Not wanting to indicate an undeclared major, she wrote down "nursing" and decided to look into it. Talking with other nurses, she became interested in the profession and found those with whom she spoke were very proud of their work and had much respect for what they did. Friends and family encouraged her and indicated their respect for the nursing profession. She entered a BSN program.

Jane J. realized that she was someone who needed to interact with people. She chose nursing when faced with the need to declare a major in college. She added the following:

> Being a nice Jewish girl, I never really had a desire to have a career. I always figured I would get married and be a good Jewish wife and mother. My parents wanted me to have an education that would allow me the luxury of being independent. . . . With nursing I would always have something to fall back on. That is how it started.

Jane believed that her father helped influence her decision when he told her that with a nursing background she could always be independent.

Other respondents pointed out that nursing was a second choice because they would have liked to have studied medicine but were unable to do so. Nonetheless, they went on to enjoy successful and rewarding careers in nursing with families who supported their efforts.

Alice A., a young woman who described herself as a single parent from a Conservative Jewish background, had wanted to study medicine but settled on nursing. Her family supported her decision, and she never heard anybody say "not for a Jewish woman."

Lauren L. said that she chose nursing, although she probably would have preferred to study medicine. At that time (the early 1950s) nursing was one of the few career choices open to women. Her parents were very supportive and encouraged her to go into nursing. Her mother was also a nurse who had completed her education in the 1920s and then worked as a public health nurse in the health department.

Annette A. recalled that, in 1954, when she was 17 years old, she changed her mind about entering a premed program and entered nursing school instead. Her cousin, Catherine C., whom she admired, had also chosen to study nursing. Her family was quite supportive concerning her decision.

Deborah D. completed nursing school in 1977. She had wanted to study medicine but chose nursing instead. Her parents knew that whatever she chose would be all right. She heard from one family member, "Oh, you're too smart to be a nurse." However, her parents were comfortable with her decision, and she had their support.

In Lillian L.'s words, "I always wanted to be a doctor, but I was female, Jewish, and poor. I didn't want to be a teacher or a secretary." So she went into a school of nursing in the 1940s and joined the U.S. Cadet Nurse Corps. Indeed, she had heard that "Nursing is not for a Jewish girl." But because we were at war, she believed her mother couldn't really say, "No." "She was very patriotic, and she was very proud when I finished," said Lillian.

Some of the respondents cited the influence of their mothers and other women in their families or social structure as an influence on their decision to enter nursing. Celia C. (below) referred to a teacher who had taken an interest in her. Helen H. described her family in terms of a strong matriarchal pattern. They also found general family approval in their career choice.

Amy A. was a young nurse in her early 20s who decided on a nursing career at the age of 16. She said she made the decision because of "my love for people, flexibility, and my own personal need to help others." Amy came from a strong Jewish background. Her mother, a nurse who "never complained about her job and loved it," wholeheartedly supported Amy's decision but had "never tried to talk me into it. My family and friends were very proud of me and my choice."

Celia C. had finished nursing school in 1928. At the age of 16, she had been encouraged by a teacher in high school to enroll in nursing. She said, "My mother always wanted one of her daughters to be a nurse. My father didn't want me to go away from home." But her teacher persuaded him to allow her to enter nursing school.

Ariela A. tells her story in these words:

> I was 12 years old when I decided to become a nurse. My mother and my grandmother greatly influenced my decision to become a nurse. My

mother was open to whatever I wanted to do but showed obvious joy when I told her I was considering nursing. My maternal grandmother, who was born in Russia and had no formal schooling, was a highly intelligent and competent woman whose own mother had been a "peasant midwife." My grandmother also possessed great skills as an untrained nurse, and many people sought her out for her "nursing" expertise. Local doctors would ask her to assist in many procedures, including "dropping ether" when they operated on someone in the home on the kitchen table. She was absolutely delighted when I told her I was considering nursing. She never pushed me, just showed delight. My father . . . was always very proud and full of encouragement for whatever I wanted to do.

Ariela said she had two older cousins—nurses for whom the family had great respect—and they seemed pleased by her career choice. However, Ariela reported that "I also have an older cousin who's a physician, and he openly derided my choice, not understanding why I either didn't want to become a physician or simply get married and have kids!"

Helen H. was a young woman in her early 40s who knew she wanted to be a nurse from the time she started high school. At age 12, she had worked as a volunteer in programs for developmentally disabled children and later as a "candy striper." She described herself as coming from a matriarchal family—on her mother's side, three generations of women successfully ran businesses. Her parents supported her decision to enter nursing. One of her cousins also went into nursing. One negative view came from a teacher who commented about "a waste of a brilliant math mind" because she was very good in mathematics and physics.

Annabelle A. wrote the following:

I was 18 years old when I decided that nursing was the career for me. It was 1940! I am now 71 years old. My aunt, who is 96 years old now, decided that I would make a good nurse, as little as I was. I was the one who went to the houses of the sick or bereaved relatives to offer them comfort and help!

Although no one tried to discourage Annabelle from going into nursing, her mother had doubts according to Annabelle. "She thought it would be a difficult job for me, but I proved her to be wrong!"

Respondents quoted in the next segment attributed their motivation to enter nursing to observing or receiving exemplary nursing care at an earlier period of their lives. The nurses they met inspired them.

Bella B., at age 85, looked back on her life as a wife, mother, daughter, sister, and nurse. As a child, Bella had been impressed by her experiences with nurses and nursing. At age 9, while visiting her sister who was hospitalized, Bella observed the nurses, and she liked what she saw. When she was 12 years old, she developed scarlet fever and was hospitalized for 1 month in the local communicable disease hospital. In high school she selected courses that would prepare her for nursing school. Her father thought that she was not "cut out for" nursing but did not discourage her, and he seemed proud of her when she finished the program in 1930. "I talked my sister into going into nursing," she said. Later, her daughter also went into nursing.

Lynn L., in her 40s, remembered being impressed by nurses when she was hospitalized for a tonsillectomy at the age of 3. Some years later, she reported thinking that she "wanted to be a doctor," but her mother demurred. She said that while she was in high school she decided on a career in nursing and her family did not object—her aunt was a nurse. Years later, she accomplished her earlier goal when she became a doctor by earning a DNSc—Doctor of Nursing Science—degree at the age of 43.

As a young child during the Depression, Elaine E. said she dreamed of becoming a fashion designer, but that was out of the question. When she was 12 years old, she was hospitalized for 30 days with scarlet fever. "It was my first contact with nurses . . . and they were kind and understanding. . . . The starched, crisp uniforms impressed [me] . . . I was hooked!" She said her mother was pleased when she decided to enter nursing school. To pay her tuition, her father asked his employer to lend him money, which he "paid back at the rate of $5.00 a week from his paycheck." She said other relatives and friends were less congenial, believing that nursing was demeaning and dirty work. One comment was, "The only positive thing that could come of [being a nurse is] to snag a doctor for a husband and become a rich society matron."

Bonnie B. reported that she had completed a baccalaureate program in 1976. As a small child, when she had been hospitalized, she was very much "impressed by a young nursing student who was very warm and caring." While in high school, she began to think about a career in nursing. When she went to college, she had an undeclared major but took courses that would move her into nursing. Although members of her family would ask her if she wouldn't rather be a doctor, her parents supported her decision to become a nurse.

Carolyn C. said that as a child, she had experienced serious illness, which imbued her with a desire to become a nurse. Her older sister had gone into nursing, and that was an inspiration to her. About one-half of her fellow students in nursing school were Jewish. Some described how their parents had not wanted them to go into nursing because "carrying bedpans was not for a Jewish girl." When she enrolled in nursing school, she had the full support of her mother who placed a high value on education.

Gloria G. was a young woman who earned her nursing school diploma in 1980 and said she became interested in nursing while working with several nursing students as a nursing assistant in a nursing home. They were a close group and she was greatly influenced by them. Her father wanted her to be a nurse because he believed that would help her have economic security. Her mother had wanted to be a nurse in her youth but "it was felt that she was not strong enough. Nobody tried to talk me out of [being a nurse], and I didn't realize it was something that Jewish women did not readily do."

The experiences described by the group of Jewish women in the foregoing narratives were overwhelmingly positive, and, clearly, they belie the persistent notion that Jewish families did not have a positive regard for nursing as a suitable career. The next group of narratives shows additional experiences that help to dispel this myth.

Her Mother Said, "Ugh!" Now She Says, With Pride, "It's My Daughter, The Nurse!"

The following narratives characterize situations in which reactions of parents, other family members, or friends were neutral, mixed, or even negative. Nonetheless, even in this group, the overall outcomes were positive. That is, situations that started out as negative eventually became positive. Parents were supportive and proud of "My daughter, the nurse."

Within the first segment are stories of several nurses who were firm in their convictions that they wanted to become nurses. As noted in some of the narratives, they were motivated by high ideals. In some instances, when they encountered opposition from one or both of their parents, they tried to convince them of their resolve. In other situations, they temporarily set their goals aside and came back to them in later years. In time, parents were won over, accepting their daughters' decisions and showing pride in their accomplishments.

Anita A. recalled at age 50 that she was inspired to go into nursing when she was a teenage volunteer at a local hospital. "It was here at the hospital that nursing became a reality and I thought that this might be what I would like to do." Two of her neighbors were nurses, and she was influenced by them. Anita's father encouraged and supported her in her decision to enter nursing. Her mother said, "Ugh, Jewish girls don't do that and you'll have to empty bedpans." But in the end she was proud of her daughter, the nurse.

Andrea A. reported completing a collegiate nursing program in 1985 and described her mother as being opposed to her decision to choose a career in nursing. Andrea said, "It took me a long time to convince her how much I wanted to do this." She said her friends had been neutral, but "when I graduated, they were very supportive."

Jean J. was 54 years old when she recalled that as a teenager she had been a candy striper at a city hospital in New York and wanted to become a nurse after completing high school. She said, "My parents thought it was outrageous, 'No daughter of mine will carry bedpans,' roared my father." Jean married, had a child, moved to another state, and in her late 30s became a licensed practical nurse (LPN). She then earned an associate degree in nursing and became an RN. She says her parents are now "quite proud of my being a nurse."

Sylvia S., a nationally and internationally prominent nursing leader, spoke about her decision in the mid-1940s to pass up medical school for a baccalaureate nursing program. Sylvia's parents had assumed that she would become a physician like her paternal aunt. They were very much opposed to her decision to become a nurse. Her aunt was called in to mediate the situation and reassured them that "as long as she's going to college, don't worry." She said her parents calmed down, but it took her mother many years to admit that she was a nurse without prefacing the remark with, "She's a professor" or "she's a PhD."

Hannah H. reported that she was born in a Central European country, from which she escaped in 1939 following Hitler's invasion. She settled in the United States in 1946 after the end of World War II. Hannah was drawn to nursing after the events that she had witnessed in Europe. She said that when she announced her decision to enter nursing school, "My mother was horrified [thinking] only nuns and ex-prostitutes go into nursing . . . but when she found out that I was at a university she changed her mind."

Other respondents, who were intent on becoming nurses, encountered similar forms of opposition from one or both parents. As with Nora N., whose cousin was a nurse, many had cherished their ambitions from the time that they were very young. Dale D. pointed out that her mother, who had always wanted to be a nurse, was very supportive, but her father disapproved. Betty B. and her two sisters went into nursing despite their father's opposition. However, in many instances, the opposing parties were won over.

Nora N. recalled that she wanted to be a nurse from the time that she was a young child. She had a cousin who was a nurse, and her aunt's friend was a nurse. When she told her parents what choice she had made, her father was adamantly opposed. He had a very negative impression of nursing and, in fact, had forbidden her older sister to go into nursing. Eventually Nora, along with her aunt's friend and their family doctor, succeeded in wearing down his opposition, and he gave his permission for Nora "to go in training" at a Jewish hospital, which she completed in 1950.

Julia J. reported growing up in a small city during the Depression. She entered nursing school 1 year after she had finished high school. She said her mother was supportive and "sacrificed for me to go into nursing. My father felt that it was not for a Jewish girl and he did not want me to be a bedpan carrier, but he . . . signed for me to go in." She completed her program in 1942.

Eva E. said that when she wanted to go into nursing in the late 1920s her immigrant parents were opposed to the idea, but after she completed her program at a Jewish hospital school they were very proud of her.

Diane D. completed a diploma nursing program at a Jewish hospital school in 1966. She said:

> I was the first one in my family to be a nurse. I
> don't know where the motivation came from; in

7th grade I was very sure that was what I wanted.
I remember talking to my mother who was one
of eight children and had wanted to study nursing
but had to go to work during the Depression.

Diane reports that her father, however, did not approve until he
saw her at the capping ceremony, "and then he was very proud."

Dale D., age 50, is a teacher and scholar in nursing. She said, "I
always wanted to be a nurse. . . . My father was very negative. He
thought that a Jewish girl should never be a nurse. You could be
a teacher, a secretary, but not a nurse." On the other hand, Dale's
mother, who had always wanted to be a nurse, was very supportive.

Betty B., now in her 70s, wrote, "I was 13 years old when the
notion to be a nurse came to me." Betty was one of three sisters
who became nurses. All had entered nursing school despite their
father's opposition.

When Edith E. was in her late 20s she reported that she had
decided on a career in nursing while in high school. Her parents'
reaction was not enthusiastic—her father thought that it was a
dirty job. However, they did not try to stop her, and they allowed
her to make her own decision. They supported her, and as she progressed they were proud of her, bragging about "My daughter, the
nurse."

The segment which follows includes remarks by several respondents whose parents or families were somewhat skeptical about
their daughters' intention to become nurses and doubted their abil-
ity to meet the demands of the nursing programs. As with Dorothy
D., they either underestimated the daughters' determination, or as
with Josie J., they were overprotective.

When in her 70s, Dorothy D. recalled that her family did not
approve of her entering nursing school in the mid-1940s, but they
did not discourage her. They underestimated her determination,
and they thought that she was undisciplined. Despite these obstacles, she completed her program with honors. She went on to a
varied and interesting nursing career, which she successfully com-
bined with her family responsibilities.

Gladys G., a graduate of a Jewish hospital nursing school,
explained that when she was 16—in the early 1940s—not too
many options existed for young women; she did not know too
much about nursing but thought it was attractive. Her family questioned her decision. "The work isn't clean," they said, and they
considered her to be a "spoiled kid," but they supported her deci-

sion. She completed nursing school and went on to serve in the military. Years later, her daughter, who became a nurse in Israel, was asked, "Why do you want to become a nurse? You're such a smart girl."

Beatrice B., who holds a very responsible position, reported that she had completed a basic baccalaureate program and went on to earn master's and doctoral degrees. When she entered nursing school, people believed that she would not finish. However, her parents were supportive, and they wanted her to study in a collegiate program. A maternal aunt was shocked that her mother would allow her to become a nurse and said, "A Jewish girl to carry bedpans?" When friends ask, she says "I am a nurse," and her parents always add, "She's not just a nurse."

Josie J. said that she finished nursing school in 1955. She added, "My parents were not supportive—they were somewhat overprotective and the exposure to [sickness] was not what they wanted for me. Of course, when I graduated, they were very proud." Now when her 85-year-old parents introduce her to their friends, they also add "and she is a registered nurse."

Several women considered that a career in nursing would offer economic security. Louise L., for example, turned to nursing when she realized that she could not afford to go to college, and although her parents' views were negative, they did not try to dissuade her. Opposition was not always easy to overcome, as, for example, with Esther E.'s mother, who would not yield; Esther's future husband, however, was very supportive. World War II and the accompanying surge of patriotism sometimes helped to break down opposition, as with Florence F. below.

Louise L. reported that she was 17 years old when:

> I decided to become a nurse; to my parents the image was menial—bedpans, enemas. But they did not try to dissuade me. Others thought it was unselfish and caring. None of that affected my decision, which was based on economics. . . . This was a way to further my education and look forward to a paying position; I had wanted to be a teacher but could not afford college.

Louise's sister was already in nursing school at a Jewish hospital, and that is where she decided to enroll. Louise completed her training in 1943 and went on to serve in the military in World War II.

Esther E. completed a BSN program in 1975. She said "I was not someone who had 'always wanted to be a nurse.' It was by process of elimination—I didn't know what else to do." For 9 months she had watched her father dying of lung cancer and had observed the nurses at their work. She became interested in nursing. "Nursing was a known, stable profession—a guaranteed job. That's what I was looking for." Her mother was totally opposed to the idea, "We had bitter arguments about it." However she reports that her boyfriend (future husband) was extremely supportive.

Rosalyn R. was a young woman in her early 30s when she explained that her "decision to become a nurse was primarily related to future job opportunities . . . my father was resistant to the idea because he did not think it was a job for a 'nice Jewish girl.'" His objections, however, were overridden by the fact that one must "go to college and get a degree in 'something.'"

Martha M. was a young woman who had completed a BSN program in 1987. She said she had a practical reason when she chose nursing—it seemed to assure a secure economic future. Her father was supportive. Her mother tried to dissuade her, "she has the dated version of bedpans, etc."

Florence F. reported that in the spring of 1945 during World War II, she decided to become a nurse.

> I was in my 3rd year of college. My grandmother was somewhat embarrassed by my decision . . . nursing wasn't quite acceptable for a Jewish girl . . . it was considered a menial job. [My mother] agreed to my studying to be a nurse. [She was] very patriotic—so that also convinced her that I should study nursing.

Florence completed a BSN program in 1948.

For some respondents, nursing school had to compete with medical school. Mindy M. is an example of a woman whose family would have preferred that she go into medicine. Some women said their first choice had been for a career in medicine. When they found that medical school was out of their reach, they turned to nursing, often encountering derisive or negative family reactions that had to be overcome. Some obtained advanced academic degrees and became very successful in their careers.

Mindy M. reported that she completed a baccalaureate nursing program in 1981. Her family did not see nursing in its broadest potential, and they challenged her by saying, "Why don't you want to be a doctor?" But they did not try to dissuade her.

Connie C. said she received her diploma in nursing in 1948. She went to nursing school because medical school was out of the question. Her father would have preferred that she do something else stating, "Nursing is not for a Jewish girl." Her mother, however, was supportive. Connie joined the U.S. Cadet Nurse Corps in nursing school.

Beverly B. said she went into nursing in the early 1940s. At first she had aspired to a career in medicine, but a combination of life events made this impossible. She joined the U.S. Cadet Nurse Corps and enrolled in the diploma program of a prestigious, urban hospital nursing school. Her immediate and extended family said that nursing was ". . . not good enough for a bright person like you." Beverly eventually completed her basic nursing preparation in a university program where she received her baccalaureate degree and had an exciting, rewarding career in the course of which she also earned her master's and doctoral degrees.

Donna D. is a prominent leader in nursing education. She reported that a career in nursing was not her first choice; she decided to enroll in nursing school after she was unable to get into medical school. Although her parents did not think that a young Jewish girl should become a nurse, they did not object to her enrolling in a collegiate nursing program. They financially supported her education, including her master's and doctoral programs, although her father asked, "Why do you need a master's degree to carry bedpans?"

Terry T. said she completed her baccalaureate program in 1978. She had switched to nursing after she had become discouraged about her chances of getting into medical school. "I viewed this switch as simply a way to ensure employment before I applied to medical school." There was no resistance from her family members, but they were not particularly supportive.

This last segment of respondents includes those who described a variety of motivations for choosing nursing. Lenore L., who was not sure what she would do, found her parents receptive when she chose nursing, but two other family members were negative and tried to influence her parents. Ida I. was impressed by her experience with public health nurses, but her parents were negative. Laura L., who was inspired to go into nursing by a romantic novel, upset her father and her large extended family, but she had the support of her mother and her grandfather. Deena D. was an immigrant who chose nursing after having tried and rejected other types of work, but her family was very negative. Nursing was not Francine F.'s first choice nor did it meet with the approval of her immigrant parents, but her future husband and his Americanized family helped change their attitude.

Lenore L., a retired school nurse, reported that she had not really been sure about what she wanted to do but thought she might like to be a nurse. Her parents were receptive, but she had two aunts who thought that nursing "was not for a Jewish girl." At first, they tried to dissuade Lenore's parents from giving their support, but they had friends who were in nursing, and as time went on, they were more accepting of her choice. In addition, Lenore's family physician was very supportive, and he encouraged her to enter a Jewish hospital nursing school. She served in the military during World War II and had a very successful career as a school nurse.

Ida I. sent an autobiographical sketch that had appeared in her alumni organization newsletter in 1992, when she was 80 years old. Ida said that she had entered a university nursing school in the 1930s after she had worked in a health department where she had observed and been impressed by the public health nursing staff. Her parents had considered nurses as being comparable to domestic servants until she persuaded them of the credibility of a university program where "nursing was now considered an art and professional training was needed." Ida won her parents over, she financed her own education, and she was the first Jewish nurse to apply for entrance to that school (Lane, 1992).

Deena D. reported that she came to the United States from Russia when she was about 10 years old. "At age 21, I didn't like being a teacher, or a dental assistant, although I had gone to school for both [professions]." She wanted to study medicine, "but my doctor uncle, who was the patriarch of our family . . . said it wasn't for a Jewish woman." Her family viewed nursing negatively, "The attitude toward nurses was that they were servants— but I wanted to take care of the sick and I didn't see it their way. I saw it as a good deed." She entered a diploma nursing program at a non-Jewish hospital in the city where she lived. She completed the program in 1938 and had a satisfying and rewarding career.

Laura L. said that when she was a young teenager, she was inspired to become a nurse by seeing a romantic movie. Members of her large, extended family were upset when she announced her decision to enter nursing school. She had the support of her mother, who was a very retiring person, but her father's view was that "a girl should study business and work until she gets married." Her grandfather, fortunately, was extremely supportive, and he paid her fees. When she finished nursing school, her parents were thrilled.

Francine F. completed a BSN program in the early 1970s. She said nursing was not her first choice, and when she decided to become a nurse, her parents objected. On the other hand, her future husband and his family were very encouraging and supportive; for them "[becoming a nurse] was an okay thing to do." Francine said that her parents were immigrants while her husband's parents were born in America and were "looked up to" by her parents. Thus, her parents toned down their objections. After she became a nurse, her parents "were thrilled; they were very proud of me."

Most of the women in this group indicated that for them a career in nursing was their first choice while for some it was a second choice. Respondents in this group had reported neutral, mixed, or even negative views toward becoming a nurse. Nonetheless, most of these women essentially had family support and parents who generally managed to resolve their negative views. Ultimately, many had glowing expressions of pride for "My daughter, the nurse." The next group of respondents is made up of those who experienced strong unresolved negative reactions. Included in some of the narratives were discussions of how these negative reactions were handled.

"I Signed Up, Then Told My Parents"

Despite some hurtful reactions from their families (as with Naomi N. and Pauline P.), respondents in this group coped well and proceeded to have satisfying careers. Ruth R. ran away from home, Rhoda R. graduated at the top of her class, and Rena R. became a distinguished nursing educator. Bluma B., who lived to 109, spoke glowingly about her nursing days.

Naomi N. reported that she was 18 years old and just out of high school when she told her parents that she wanted to be a nurse. She said:

> My father felt all nurses were loose women and all they did was empty bedpans. My mother firmly said she would not want me to pursue nurs-

ing because it was a Christian job—no decent Jewish girl became a nurse.

For the next year Naomi went to work in an office. Meanwhile, she learned that the U.S. Cadet Nurse Corps had been established and that she could enter nursing through that program. "I signed up, then told my parents. I don't remember them being too upset."

Melanie M., who had just turned 40, reported that she entered nursing in her mid-20s almost by default. She had a negative image of nursing and had wanted to study medicine. Her mother, who was an RN, was against her decision to go into nursing; her father, on the other hand, considered nursing more appropriate than medicine. After graduation, she went into psychiatric nursing. She did not pursue a career in medicine because "I discovered I wanted to care for people and not diseases." She also discovered that being a nurse from a college program gave her greater credibility than that which her mother had experienced at the diploma level.

Bluma B., at the age of 102, looked back on her long life and recalled that her mother was not happy about her decision to become a nurse. She grew up on a farm in one of the agricultural communities supported by Jacob Schiff and Baron de Hirsch to encourage immigrant Jewish families to settle outside of the large cities. At the age of 15, she left the farm to work in the city (Purmell, 1981). After a few years she began to think about becoming a nurse, and, despite objections from some members of her family, she entered a Jewish hospital school of nursing. On completing the program, she had a long and rewarding career.

Pauline P. recalled how her father, in the late 1930s, did not want her to go into nursing school. "He said, 'Don't you know you'll have to carry bedpans,' and I told him that there must be something else to this besides bedpans." She had to face many challenges in school and at one point she was ready to drop out. However, she found the courage and determination to stay on and was always happy that she made that decision. After Pauline completed nursing school, she announced her intention of volunteering for military service, and once again her father was unhappy about her decision. He said, "For the first time in my life I'm glad you were a girl and could not be drafted and you tell me you're going to volunteer?" Nevertheless, Pauline enlisted in the Army Nurse Corps during World War II and served overseas, in the Persian Gulf and in Europe, for 34 months.

Phyllis P. submitted a brief response saying that she had completed her basic nursing program in 1956. Her mother, Ruth R., now deceased, had also been a nurse, and "had to run away from home [to enter nursing school in the 1920s] because her father was so strongly opposed."

Rena R. said:

> I lived in the religious ghetto of the Lower East Side of New York. I wanted to be a nurse since the age of 2, but it was not seen as a Jewish occupation. . . . My parents were vehemently against it and I had to wait until I was 21 thereby not requiring their permission to enter nursing school.

Rena completed her program in 1968 without any help from her father, who did not change his negative view of her choice.She went on to a distinguished career as a nursing educator.

Rhoda R., who completed nursing school in 1947, said:

> My father was violently against my becoming a nurse, and the rest of the family wasn't supportive either. . . . I graduated near the top of the class.

Summary

These brief narratives embody a broad range of views and sentiments expressed by Jewish family members and friends of the respondents whenever one of the young women in their midst declared her intention of pursuing a career in nursing. There were, of course, negative reactions, some quite vehement, but, at least in the group represented here, they were in the minority. Yet, these types of comments have been regarded as "typical" among members of the Jewish community. Indeed, parental and other family opposition can be very powerful. Who knows how many young Jewish women yielded to family pressure and decided not to become nurses?

In the course of gathering information for this study, I encountered several elderly Jewish women who regretted all their lives that they gave up their desire to become nurses because of family opposition. One of them shared her story. She said that she had completed high school with honors in 1923 and wanted to go to nursing school. She described the reaction of her cousin who had become a "big doctor" and was looked up to as the patriarch of their extended immigrant family. His pronunciamento was "you don't want to be a nurse because they're all bums," a statement that speaks volumes about the family patriarch but tells nothing about nurses or nursing. His position and authority in the family were unquestioned. This woman could not go against the family's position, and she was heartbroken. The nursing profession lost a good recruit.

One cannot help but admire the women whose narratives reflect that, despite negative reactions, they had the determination to pursue their desired goal. They went on to have rewarding careers in nursing and to contribute significantly to the nursing profession.

Note that similar negative views are also expressed by members of non-Jewish families in corresponding situations. Such views about nursing cut across socio-cultural, religious, and ethnic boundaries and are fueled by a lack of understanding of what nursing is all about. To put it another way, certain stereotypes about nurses are so prevalent, that "within two sentences of being introduced to strangers, someone will mention bedpans or other cloacal references" (Diers, 1972). Such sentiments are disconcerting and have undoubtedly led to the kinds of negative reactions and experiences reported by some of the respondents.

So, how did our parents and families really feel about it? The tabulation of responses in this survey revealed fewer negative responses than positive responses on the part of Jewish parents and other family members. For the most part, they were supportive of their family members' decision to enter nursing. In effect, the results of the survey belie the firmly entrenched and virtually unshakable view, constantly reiterated, that Jewish families believe that "It is *not* for a Jewish girl." What, then, do we have here? Is this a case of "My mind is made up, don't confuse me with facts?" Is it fair and reasonable to continue to ascribe such negative reactions to a "Jewish" view of nursing? Or is this a myth that has been reinforced by repetition, and should it finally be laid to rest?

References

Diers, D. (1972). It's a good time for nursing. *Yale Alumni Magazine, 36*(3), 8- 13.

Lane, I. J. (1992, January). *Ida June 'Idie' Levin Lane '36* (Pin #193).University of Wisconsin (Madison) Nurses Alumni Organization Newsletter.

Purmell, B. B. R. (1981). *A farmer's daughter: Bluma. Los Angeles:* Hayvenhurst Publishers.

8

As Others See Us:
"I Never Experienced Anti-Semitism"
Versus
"Thank God There Are No Jews Among Us"

aving decided that "it *is* for a Jewish girl" and for the most part with the support of their parents and in some situations in defiance of their parents, and realizing that getting their hands dirty was "no big deal," and moving into a field purportedly based on "Christian principles," how did Jewish women fare when they entered nursing? What were some of their experiences? How did they come to terms with negative or mixed messages that came from the world of nursing and from the Jewish community? The women who responded to the survey about their experiences in nursing and about their personal lives addressed many issues related to these questions.

Some of the issues, which they discussed, are relevant to all women and to all nurses. For example, all women and all nurses, including Jewish women and Jewish nurses, will find relevance in issues such as:

1. choosing a career pattern,
2. making decisions about working while children are small,
3. formulating attitudes about the women's movement,
4. putting forth efforts to attain advanced education.

Other issues that were discussed are of special significance to Jewish women and to Jewish nurses. For example:

1. Jewish heritage, including the immigrant experience,
2. level of participation in Jewish community affairs,
3. experiences as Jewish nurses in the profes-

sional community,
4. experiences as nurses within the Jewish community.

For our purpose, let us look at the latter set of issues as addressed by the respondents in the survey. In this chapter, the discussion will be focused on what the respondents had to say about their experiences:

1. in the professional community—with a particular focus on the problem of anti-Semitism, and
2. within the Jewish community—including encounters with anti-nurse sentiments.

Thus, the emphasis in this chapter will be on seeing ourselves as others see us. The next chapter will describe how we see ourselves within the context of our Jewish heritage and its impact on our situation in nursing.

A search of nursing literature indicated almost nothing that speaks to these points, except for a very poignant statement by one of America's most prominent nurses, Dr. Ingeborg Mauksch. Mauksch, who went into nursing after she came to this country as a refugee from Nazism just before World War II, had this to say (Schorr & Zimmerman, 1988):

> It is appropriate here to raise the issue of being Jewish in a predominantly non-Jewish occupation. There are relatively few Jewish nurses in the United States—certainly in fewer numbers than to be representative of the United States' Jewish population. I feel that I have always had the respect of my peers and colleagues regarding my observance of Jewish holidays and the perspective on world politics, which obviously reflects my Jewish point of view. I am always identified as a Jew and feel that I have been respected as such. Likewise, that feeling enhances the respect I have for my professional colleagues and my profession. Nurses have always proclaimed to be blind to ethnic differences but have not always been expected to act that way. I am glad to say that my experiences as a minority in virtually every position that I have had

on the local, state, and national levels in nursing
have been positive (p. 259).

Another published reference to one's experience in nursing vis-a-vis her Jewish background came from the distinguished nurse theorist and educator, Myra Levine (Schorr & Zimmerman, 1988). Levine described how, in the early 1940s, she was denied admission to the Michael Reese Hospital School of Nursing, adding that "although it was funded by the Jewish Federation of Chicago, the director of nursing at the school maintained a careful quota of Jewish students" (p. 219).

The text that follows shows how the women who responded to the survey experienced these and other points of special relevance to Jewish nurses. The first group of narratives came from nurses who (a) did not encounter serious difficulties because of their Jewish background, or (b) satisfactorily resolved situations that might otherwise have been problematic.

"Anti-Semitism Was Never a Problem"

Within the first segment of this group of narratives are those from respondents for whom anti-Semitism was not a problem. These nurses were from different parts of the country, from various nursing programs, and from different time periods.

Alice A., who is now in her mid-30s, grew up in one of the southern states and studied nursing at a university there. Alice said, "There were six Jewish students in my class; anti-Semitism was never a problem." Nor did Elizabeth E., Gloria G., Gail G., Helen H., Lauren L., and Lorna L., all of whom lived in one of the mid-Atlantic states, experience anti-Semitism. Gloria and Lauren studied at Jewish hospital schools of nursing while the others were in baccalaureate degree programs. Elizabeth earned her BSN as a second degree and Lorna studied nursing as a second career.

Susan S., who had not experienced anti-Semitism, said, "My peers have been respectful and curious asking about customs, traditions, etc." Similar to Susan's experience, Amy A. had not experienced anti-Semitism and also found her peers respectful. In 1990, Amy graduated from a Baptist hospital school of nursing in one of the southern states. She said she was:

. . . the only Jewish student in the school of about
600-700 students . . . the other students were

never afraid to ask me questions about my faith. My mother [who is also a nurse] and I participated in the Baptist Student Union during the holiday times so that we could teach the other students the difference between our faiths. It worked out well. I was never excluded from activities and knew I was welcome at all functions. Sometimes during Rosh Hashanah and Yom Kippur, it became difficult if I had a test on one of those days. Eventually I could take the test on a different day.

Brenda B. reported she had never directly experienced anti-Semitism. "If it was around me, I was not aware." Concerning Brenda's work in a Roman Catholic hospital she said, "I do not feel singled out because of my religion." Nora N. also worked at a Roman Catholic hospital and did not experience anti-Semitism. Nora recalled a long and happy career in nursing. She had to overcome her father's objections to nursing and she declared that her time spent as a nursing student in a hospital program was "one of the happiest times of my life." At the hospital where Nora worked, "the staff nurses were glad to have me on the staff because I would work every Christmas . . . so they could have the time off."

Beth B. held a high administrative position on a nursing education faculty to which a large number of Jewish members were appointed. "They were not deliberately chosen because they were Jewish. They're smart, work hard, are career-oriented, manage their personal lives and jobs, and do very well." Beth reported not experiencing any unpleasantness with regard to anti-Semitism.

Within the next segment of narratives, several respondents reported that they did not encounter anti-Semitism within their professional practice but described unpleasant experiences that occurred in their lives before they entered nursing.

Deena D., now quite elderly, lived through pogroms in czarist Russia as a young child before coming to the United States. She did not indicate any experience with anti-Semitism throughout her nursing career.

Lillian L. grew up in a traditional Jewish home in one of the southern states in an area where there were few other Jewish families. She once witnessed a cross-burning. Her best friend was the daughter of a Presbyterian minister. Lillian went to a Jewish hospital school of nursing in a mid-Atlantic state. She reported never encountering anti-Semitism in her professional life. In fact, when Lillian heard her Jewish classmates speak about their experiences with anti-Semitism she believed they were exaggerating. "I thought that my Jewish colleagues . . . attributed [any] criticism directed at them as anti-Semitism."

Emily E., in her early 30s, reported that while she was in nursing school, she did not experience anti-Semitism. Her colleagues knew that she was Jewish, and they respected her. One time, however, when Emily was working as a nurse's aide at a local hospital during her student days, an unpleasant incident occurred in which she overheard some nurses refer to their weekend plans for going off to the shore, ". . . where there are no Jews!"

Bonnie B. recalled anti-Semitic experiences from her childhood, but not in nursing school or in her nursing practice. "But sometimes I had difficulty getting people to understand why I needed to be off on High Holidays." She believes that the best strategies to combat anti-Semitism come from empowerment and from the realization that we "don't have to take it."

Other strategies to combat anti-Semitism are cited in the next segment; respondents discuss various proactive measures that have worked for them. Martha M. and Donna D. were in positions of influencing policy and sought ways to promote dialog and to foster change in avoiding insensitive or thoughtless expressions of anti-Semitism. Pearl P., Eileen E., Evelyn E., and Edith E. found ways to meet troublesome situations head-on, to clear the air, and to prevent repeated unpleasantness. Beverly B. expressed appreciation for the establishment of the Hadassah Nurses Councils with their potential for creating solidarity and a support system. Sylvia S. emphasized the importance of establishing a demeanor of openness. Sylvia and Lynn also identified an anti-nurse bias among their Jewish acquaintances.

Martha M. said she has not experienced anti-Semitism at work. Her head nurse belonged to a synagogue. Her colleagues formed a group that encouraged an open exchange of cultural experiences.

Donna D. is a distinguished nursing educator with a doctoral degree. Although she did not experience anti-Semitism as a student or as a professor, Donna said she has encountered a great deal of ignorance and insensitivity. "I am outspoken and assertive. I keep an eye out for the Jewish students; being in charge, I don't allow exams on the High Holy Days. I have had to educate my colleagues and make them more sensitive."

Edith E. recalled only one anti-Semitic incident in her work, with which she dealt immediately and to her satisfaction. Similarly, Eileen E. pointed out that, while she did not feel that she was a target of anti-Semitism in work situations, she had heard hurtful comments and said, "I have learned to be more assertive when hearing these remarks, which has helped cut down on repeated incidents." Pearl P. said she did not encounter anti-Semitism in the Jewish hospital school that she attended in the 1930s. Later, at a city hospital school where she taught, she felt an undercurrent of anti-Semitism, which she described as "nothing openly showing but . . . it was evident in small ways. I held my own as a Jew and spoke out when necessary."

Evelyn E. reported that she encountered prejudice against Jews, sometimes from patients. She added, "As a younger person I kept it quiet. Now I have the sophistication and knowledge to handle it in a very professional manner." Evelyn does not have any problems scheduling her work so that she is free on the Sabbath and on the Jewish holidays. Similarly, Francine F. said that when she was in nursing school, she was able to negotiate excused absences on certain Jewish holidays, even though her request would create some confusion for her instructors, because other Jewish students did not ask to be excused on those days!

Beverly B. said she had to deal with some anti-Semitic experiences in her nursing career. She welcomed the movement for the creation of nurses councils through Hadassah and referred to the young Jewish women in nursing today "who talk up . . . and have a strong Jewish connection."

Sylvia S. completed her nursing program in the late 1940s through the U.S. Cadet Nurse Corps. She completed graduate studies and earned a doctorate in the mid-1960s. She said, "Choosing nursing was luck. I loved every minute of it." She discussed her experiences with anti-Semitism by saying:

> One of my techniques was always to be very careful about my openness. I'd announce that I'm Jewish, i.e., I'd include it in my conversation. I learned this because I had a number of experiences in school. . . . There were no anti-Semitic experiences in the work world. . . . If they did occur, my nature was to put them out of my mind, because I have had a wonderfully positive experience.

What Sylvia said she did find more troublesome were expressions of disdain for nursing that she encountered in what she described as "upper-middle-class Jewish" social settings.

Lynn L. said she had not experienced overt anti-Semitism in her professional work. "I don't hide the fact that I'm Jewish, but I don't announce it either." Lynn said she also believes that some Jewish women look down on nursing.

The women in the previous segment of respondents claimed that they had not encountered serious expressions of anti-Semitism. However, they described experiences that arose from ignorance or insensitivity. Their responses illustrated how they individually adopted ways to cope with these types of anti-Semitic expressions. Beverly B. also alluded to the potential for creating a group mechanism of support through the Hadassah Nurses Councils. Sylvia S. and Lynn L. pointed to what they characterized as Jewish anti-nursing sentiments. The segment that follows is focused on those nurses who felt a sense of isolation but did not speak out when confronted with insensitivity or insensibility of unthinking individuals.

Esther E. gave up clinical nursing practice and has been working in utilization review. She enjoyed nursing but it had become very stressful. Esther had worked in a Jewish hospital, where she did not encounter anti-Semitism. Unlike Brenda B. and Nora N. (above), Esther ran into some unpleasant incidents during her period of employment at a Catholic hospital, and she recalled that at that time, she was "too shy to speak up."

Emma E. completed her diploma program at a Jewish hospital school of nursing about 40 years ago. Although Emma said she never experienced anti-Semitism in nursing, she recalled that often "as the only Jew in some of these settings I had the feeling that my religion was noticed and I was considered an oddity. I was expected to explain myself on many occasions." Similarly, Diane D., Leslie L., and Fern F. had indicated that they had not experienced anti-Semitism in nursing. However, Diane said that at times she felt a sense of isolation, while Leslie added, "Sometimes I heard comments, but I ignored them," and Fern stated that many times she felt like an outsider, especially around the non-Jewish holidays.

Anita A. reported completing a diploma program in a non-Jewish hospital nursing school in 1961. She was the only Jewish student in a class of 80. Anita has often been the only Jewish nurse in settings where she was employed and has worked nearly every

Christmas and Easter for the past 30 years. She denies having experienced blatant anti-Semitism, other than occasional stereotypical remarks, but admits that she does like to work with Jewish patients.

Rita R., a retired school nurse in her 70s, recalled her experiences in nursing school at a non-Jewish hospital. Rita and another classmate were the only two Jewish students in their class and were considered "different" by the other young women, which gave rise to some unpleasantness. Rita did not experience anti-Semitism among the instructors or the medical staff. After she completed nursing school, Rita took a position at a Jewish hospital where nearly all of the staff were Jewish. "Not having to worry about someone saying 'you're different' was a good feeling." She enlisted in the military during World War II and served in the Pacific zone and did not report experiencing anti-Semitism in the military.

Like Rita, nurses in the next segment referred to their military service and their wartime experiences, generally, in a positive way. They indicated they did not encounter anti-Semitism in their professional lives.

Louise L., a retired school nurse, had followed her older sister in entering a Jewish hospital school of nursing. (Louise's sister had originally applied to a non-Jewish hospital school, which had denied her admission with the following comment by the director, "We think that you would be happier at the Jewish Hospital.") After completing nursing school, Louise worked at the Jewish hospital where she had studied and then served in the military during World War II. "I never experienced any anti-Semitism nor did I ever feel any in my professional life," she said.

Lorraine L. indicated that she had studied at a Jewish hospital school of nursing where most of her classmates were Jewish. During World War II, she served in the military as a flight nurse. She said, ". . . we learned how to be on the planes and to calm the men who were anxious." Lorraine said she never experienced anti-Semitism. "Maybe I was very fortunate." Lorraine added that when she returned to civilian life, she went into school nursing in the role of counseling, which she greatly enjoyed.

Rachel R. stated she had completed a diploma program in a Jewish hospital nursing school in 1950. She served in the U.S. Air Force Nurse Corps from 1953 to 1973. "I developed many good friendships," said Rachel, and she added that she was not aware of anti-Semitism.

Carolyn C. reported completing a diploma program at a Jewish hospital school of nursing in 1943 and going into the Navy Nurse Corps. Carolyn said she never experienced anti-Semitism in nursing school or in the Navy. "The most anti-Semitic person I met in the Navy was a Jewish doctor; it was an unpleasant experience, and I blotted out most of it."

Elaine E. said she enlisted in the Army Nurse Corps soon after her graduation in the early 1940s and served at home and in the Philippines. Elaine referred to only one anti-Semitic incident in her nursing experience, which occurred while training nursing aides in a Roman Catholic hospital.

Rose R. reported completing a diploma program in the 1930s at a municipal hospital nursing school in a large city where two girls in a class of 98 were Jewish. She served in the military in World War II, where she had only non-Jewish friends, and never experienced anti-Semitism. "I always used to tell people right off the bat that I was Jewish."

Looking at this first group of narratives, we see that most of the respondents believed they did not experience overt anti-Semitism. In fact, with few exceptions, most of these respondents reported congenial experiences. The next group of respondents reflects a somewhat different array of experiences.

"Anti-Semitism Rears Its Ugly Head"

The first segment of this group continues with narratives of nurses who served in the military. Unlike their colleagues in the previous segment, these nurses delineated some ugly incidents that they had experienced.

Gladys G. served in the Navy Nurse Corps during World War II and the Korean conflict. Gladys reported anti-Semitism from some of her colleagues, one of whom referred to her as the "Jewgirl." "Another time, one of them said, 'I hate Jews' and I told her I was Jewish and her response was, 'Oh, you're different.'"

Hannah H. wrote, "I became a nurse because I wanted to do something meaningful after what happened in Europe. I have never regretted my decision." Hannah said she fled her native land in 1939, 6 months after it had been invaded by Hitler. When she finally settled in the United States, Hannah enrolled in a baccalaureate nursing program, where she was the only Jewish student during her 4 years there. "Upon arrival in the dorm, I met my classmates and one of the first sentences I heard was, "Thank God there are no Jews among us." I informed her of my religion. It did seem to make a difference to some, not to others, and I made some lifelong friendships." After completing nursing school, Hannah served in the Air Force for 2 years during the Korean War, where she recalled an anti-Semitic incident that was triggered by a superior officer. Fortunately for her, it did not have an effect on her promotion, although she was transferred to another unit where she served under a Jewish commanding officer.

Pauline P. reported that she had completed nursing school in the early 1940s at a Jewish hospital. Most of her classmates were Jewish. She went into the military and served in the Persian Gulf area. She and four other Jewish nurses in her unit were subjected to anti-Semitic barbs, "Imagine going overseas with five Jewgirls." The first chief nurse to whom they were assigned was competent and treated them fairly. The next officer behaved quite differently and treated Pauline and her Jewish colleagues unfairly.

Lenore L. said she studied at a Jewish hospital nursing school, completed her program in 1942, and did private duty nursing until she received an appointment as a school nurse. In 1945, Lenore enlisted in the Army Nurse Corps where she served for nearly 2 years. She recalled anti-Semitic incidents from her nursing school days—on the part of the director of nursing; from her military service—where she heard Jewish service personnel referred to as "kikes"; and from her experience in the school nurse service—where Jewish nurses got the worst assignments. Nonetheless, she had good friends and colleagues in the military who were not Jewish. After Lenore completed military service, she went back to school nursing, where she had a long and rewarding career.

Bernice B. reported studying at a Jewish hospital nursing school, working in public health nursing after graduation, and joining the American Red Cross. After Pearl Harbor, Bernice enlisted in the Army Nurse Corps and was sent to the Persian Gulf. In the military she experienced anti-Semitism with frequent disparaging remarks from colleagues about Jewish nurses and doctors. After being discharged from the military, Bernice resumed her career in civilian nursing where she again encountered anti-Semitism.

The open hostility depicted in the foregoing incidents was also evident in civilian settings as described in the next segment of narratives. Here we read of blatant acts of anti-Semitism that reflected some of the seamiest and vilest qualities of human behavior.

The oldest nurse in the survey, Bluma B., who was first interviewed at age 102, recalled feelings of hatred expressed to her by patients when she was a young nurse. She reported that while studying at a Jewish hospital school of nursing, she heard patients speak of Jews with animosity. Bluma said she often challenged them and asked why they harbored such feelings of hatred but that they had no rational response.

Annabelle A. described a hostile "anti-Semitic attack" in which a fellow employee had angrily declared, in her presence, that "Hitler did not kill enough Jews." This incident was brought before a union delegate meeting in which a ruling was handed down suspending this employee for 1 week with loss of pay.

Beatrice B. reported studying nursing in a collegiate program at a major university in the early 1960s. In her first year she met a young non-Jewish classmate who stared at her in disbelief saying, "I never saw a Jew before." In her nursing practice she experienced discrimination. Once when she was being interviewed for a position in a southern state, she said the interviewer "played with my name" and asked, "What kind of name is that?" In another situation she was advised by a recruiter who referred to her New York Jewish background that "I'm concerned that you would not fit in [for a position in a Midwestern state]." In Beatrice's view, quotas have existed against Jewish women wanting to go into nursing, even in schools associated with Jewish hospitals. Beatrice believes that Jewish nurses are numerically underrepresented in nursing but that "more of them go on for advanced degrees."

Rena R., a prominent nursing educator with a doctoral degree, held positions of leadership in professional organizations. Her basic nursing preparation was at a Jewish hospital diploma program. Rena reported experiencing anti-Semitism in nursing school as "vague but not palpable" and later encountered hostile, blatant anti-Semitism in nursing practice, nursing education, and professional organizations. "I remember an administrator surprised to find out that I was Jewish and said with all innocence, 'Jewish girls do not go into nursing, they don't like to get their hands dirty.'" She said she met such situations head-on, adding "I am bold, direct, opinionated, courageous . . . and knowledgeable in my convictions."

Rhoda R., retired, recalled negative experiences as a student in the late 1940s. The director of the nursing school she attended, at a city hospital on the West Coast, was openly anti-Semitic and racist. "She told me that she didn't think Jews made good nurses." Rhoda was in the U.S. Cadet Nurse Corps and after graduation attained a high score on the state board examination. She received a letter of commendation from that same director. Some of her classmates "thought it was perfectly okay to make remarks and jokes about Jews. You either fought them or pretended not to hear." Otherwise, throughout her career, she did not experience anti-Semitism. She openly discussed observance of religious holidays wherever she worked and had no difficulty getting time off to attend services.

Several nurses, as we see in the next segment, found that the issue of arranging schedules in order to observe the Sabbath, holidays, and other religious customs and rituals was often problematic. Unlike the nurses who did not experience difficulties in the first group presented earlier, the women in the following discussions ran into some unpleasant situations.

Karla K., in her mid-30s, reported experiencing difficulties as a student when she needed time off for the Jewish holidays and for "sitting shiva" after her grandfather died. At one hospital where she worked, the staff and supervisory personnel were unsympathetic to her requests for schedule adjustments around Jewish holidays, which created difficulty for her.

Cynthia C. referred to a display of insensitivity when professional nursing events are scheduled on Jewish holidays. She now takes steps to raise the consciousness of her non-Jewish colleagues when they are planning such events.

Observance of Jewish customs was always important to Abby A., who chose a Jewish hospital nursing school and completed her program in 1947. She reported the following:

> When the starting date was sent to me it was Rosh Hashanah. My mother sent an immediate message, and the date was changed ... I did have to work early on – a 7-day week, from 7:00 a.m. to 7:00 p.m., with 3 hours off. On Saturdays, I asked to have my time off from 9:00 a.m. to noon. And I would then go to synagogue. . . . The supervisor once said, "Why do you really want those hours off?" That was 47 years ago and I still bristle at the thought of it. And she was Jewish. I faced more anti-Semitism from Jews than Gentiles."

Abby's comment about the insensitivity of her Jewish supervisor calls to mind earlier comments by Sylvia S. and Lynn L., who described expressions of disdain for nursing that came from Jewish acquaintances. In the next segment, narratives describing similar situations are presented.

Barbara B. reported having a rewarding career. She did not indicate any experiences with anti-Semitism. However, in her parting comments, Barbara said:

> Being Jewish and being a nurse were difficult in the late 1950s and early 1960s. Nursing was a job that "nice Jewish girls didn't do." My mother-in-law never reconciled herself to the fact that I was a nurse, and it took my husband at least 10 years before he would tell anyone what I did.

Millie M. is known for her tireless efforts to promote the nursing profession within the Jewish community. She reported that, often, when she mingled socially with the people in her husband's medical circles, many of whom were Jewish, she avoided calling attention to the fact that she was a nurse because of nursing's negative image within that group.

Many of the insults and indignities that are inherent in the situations described so far in this group of narratives can be attributed to overt hostility and animosity. Some can be traced to ignorance, insensitivity, lack of understanding, and stereotyping, as exemplified by narratives that appear in the next segment.

Terry T. reported that when she was in nursing school, there were three Jewish students in a class of 66. After graduation in 1978, Terry went to work in a psychiatric hospital in a large Midwestern city. She said:

> There was considerable ignorance about Jewish people, but generally I was treated well. I was an "oddity" for many reasons—I was young, Jewish, white, and I had a BSN degree. I did run into anti-Semitism . . . from patients, especially those who were indigent and uneducated, occasionally from other nurses and aides who would make anti-Jewish remarks or "jokes," probably oblivious to my ethnic identity.

Harriet H. earned both associate and baccalaureate degrees in nursing and has been working as a staff nurse at a large urban hospital. She said she has experienced uncomfortable anti-Semitic incidents. "People are ignorant, with stereotyped notions of what Jewish means." Harriet never liked it when the topic of ethnic differences was brought up for discussion, believing that people should be judged as individuals and not on the basis of ethnic or religious background.

Similarly, when Toby T. was studying in the master's program, she wrote her thesis on the behavioral aspects of Reform Jews who experience illness. Toby reported that, in reviewing existing literature on the topic, she found negative, stereotypical comments about Jews. The findings of her research led to one of her conclusions, namely that "there is much written about Jews that is negative due to lack of understanding of Jews, Jewish values, and Jewish culture."

After her mother died, Jean J. experienced difficulties when she needed to take time off for *shiva*—the obligatory 7-day period of mourning after the death of a family member. Jean received demerits that were never removed from her work record. In addition, she described another instance of anti-Semitism, which she said:

> I foolishly thought was long gone. I was recently asked to "tone down my New York accent" if I could. . . . [Here] especially in rural areas where I live and work, [they] still think we have horns and maybe the Holocaust never really happened.

Dale D. earned her diploma at a Jewish hospital school of nursing. She recalled her program and school with great fondness. Of 100 students who entered the class, over half were Jewish. Having practiced nursing in many parts of the United States and in South America, Dale now holds a doctoral degree and is a renowned scholar in her field. Dale has encountered unfriendly and uninformed stereotypical comments about her religious, ethnic, and geographic background. She said that in one of the southern states, for example, "people regarded me as 'deviant' because I was from New York."

Thelma T. said she did not work for a few years because of family responsibilities, and when she resumed her career in the mid-1970s, she "encountered anti-Semitism in my work place, some overt and some that was more ignorance and insensitivity." She expressed regret at not having been more confrontational at that time, admitting that this might not have changed anything but she would have felt better about it. Presently she works as a hospice nurse and added, "I love nursing because I love people. . . . My patients and their loved ones have given me far more than I could ever give to them."

The tradition of Christianity in nursing has affected experiences reported by the nurses in the next segment of this group. The nurses who submitted these narratives described their actions and the actions of others in responding to problem situations. Melanie M., in her narrative, also referred to anti-nurse sentiments that she encountered among Jewish acquaintances.

Melanie M. said she was very much aware of the Christian emphasis on nursing and found it tiresome. She reported:

> When I have tried to raise consciousness in nurs-
> ing, I find some resistance. Hospital staff seem to
> be unaware of what Jews are in [the region of the
> country where she practices]. I've heard Jewish
> patients referred to as "heathens who need the
> word of God." I've seen staff nurses proselytize
> to very ill Jewish patients. . . . I try very hard to
> make my students aware of cultural differences.

She stated that many of her students have never met Jewish people and have many questions and misconceptions. Melanie also said:

> [I resent] so many Jews look[ing] down on Jewish
> nurses. When I'm asked what I do and say nurs-
> ing, I get the feeling of a door closing. If I say I
> am a nursing educator and work for a college, the
> response is totally different.

Bella B. entered nursing school in 1927. She said only four Jewish girls were in the class. The students were required to attend chapel and sing Christian hymns—by the way, this was a Jewish hospital nursing school! "I went to see the Director of Nursing, and I protested." After that, the Jewish girls were excused. Bella recalled several anti-Semitic incidents. Like Gladys G. above, one was an exchange with another nurse that went something like this, "These Jews! and how they act!" "Well, I'm Jewish." "Oh, but you're different." Other incidents involved patients who did not want to have a Jewish nurse.

Ida I.'s story was written in her nurses' alumni organization newsletter (Lane, 1992). She recalled one memorable incident in nursing school in connection with a tradition, in which she chose to participate, whereby students went around on Christmas morning singing carols for the patients. She said:

> It called for hours of practice and rehearsal with [a beloved instructor]. . . . An experience I still try to forget, yet remember because of the kindness of [her instructor], that occurred on an afternoon of rehearsal at the dorm. . . . As I was coming down the stairs, not yet visible to those in the lounge, I heard my name mentioned. "If Idie Levin is singing carols, I'm dropping out," a comment made by one of my classmates, seemingly because of my Jewish faith. Then came [the instructor's] response: "If Idie Levin wants to sing carols, she will and you may drop out!" I sang . . . and enjoyed it.

Deborah D. studied at a major university in a southern state. In school she did not experience overt anti-Semitism but said, "I found myself in a milieu where most of the students were Christian women who felt that this was their calling and that it was a very Christian thing to do." She said at times she felt "out of place as a member of a small minority, but not in my studies or professional work." She reported feeling secure in her Jewish background and in resolving an unpleasant situation involving a physician, who often made anti-Semitic and sexist remarks as a way of "teasing." She confronted him and refused to assist him in surgery. To her dismay, Deborah's colleagues did not support her and seemed embarrassed by her action. But the teasing stopped.

A variety of experiences is included in the next segment of respondents. For example, Roberta R., like Beatrice B. above, mentions a quota as referred to by Myra Levine (Schorr & Zimmerman, 1988). Connie C. and Rona R. target a specific hospital in which personnel were known for hostile attitudes. Other unpleasant experiences are also described.

Lisa L., who had been in nursing for about 5 years, wrote, "I have not run into any anti-Semitism besides 'jokes' here and there. I do find it difficult since there are so few Jewish nurses; we do usually know each other."

Roberta R. completed her studies at a Jewish hospital nursing school in 1944. Her perception at that time was that "only Jewish hospitals would accept us, and then they had an 'unspoken quota.'"

Connie C., now in her mid-60s, studied at a Jewish hospital school of nursing. Connie encountered anti-Semitism while working at a local community hospital, which was also targeted by Rona R. Rona described this as blatant anti-Semitism directed at Jewish patients and added, "I deal with it every day; the Jewish patients are very happy when they recognize [my] Jewish name."

Dorothy D., a graduate of a diploma school of nursing at a Jewish hospital, reported having an interesting and varied career. She experienced several unpleasant anti-Semitic situations. At one hospital where she worked, she noted that she was the only Jewish nurse they had had in 25 years. She said, "I was considered a pushy Jewish nurse because I had high expectations." Only one nurse extended a hand of friendship. Dorothy applied for a position at another hospital for which she was well qualified and said she was told, "We don't have anything for you, why don't you go over to the [local Jewish] hospital?"

Charlotte C. reported completing nursing school at a Jewish hospital in the mid-1940s. She told about an experience with anti-Semitism related to seeking a position as a nurse with an industrial firm. She said she was turned down when it was discovered that she was Jewish.

Summary

This chapter has shown "as others see us" as exemplified by the experiences of Jewish nurses in the professional community and by their experiences as nurses in the Jewish community. The respondents described negative views, such as anti-Semitism, encountered in the nursing community and expressions of anti-nurse sentiments in the Jewish community. Over one-half of the respondents (53%), who gave their accounts of the occurrence or non-occurrence of anti-Semitic encounters, claimed that anti-Semitism was not a troublesome issue. For instance:

- 40% indicated that they had never encountered anti-Semitism in their nursing school or in their work,
- 7% did not experience anti-Semitism, but they often felt what they described as a sense of "otherness" or "isolation" or "being an oddity,"
- 6% did not recall more than one incident of anti-Semitism in their experiences.

Among those who cited anti-Semitism as a problem (47%), their experiences reflected the unshakable grip of stereotyping among the perpetrators of such incidents. About 16% of these incidents could be characterized as overt, blatant, or hostile anti-Semitism. Annabelle A.'s episode was so egregious that it warranted disciplinary action by an employees union. A few other episodes were tinged with malice. But, most of the incidents (31%) were attributed to ignorance or insensitivity.

No identifiable pattern of occurrences emerged, that is, regional, age, cohort group, type of employment, and so on. In fact, in one area of a southern state, several nurses reported diametrically opposed types of experiences in their narratives, for example, Jean J. cited several instances of bad behavior on the part of her colleagues, while Amy A. and Alice A. were not subjected to such offensive expressions. A few respondents in other parts of the country cited unpleasant incidents generated by their own Jewish coreligionists—perhaps the most loathsome type of anti-Semitism—for example, Abby A., whose instructor challenged her after she had successfully negotiated for the time to attend Sabbath services. Some of the experiences had a slightly quirky twist, such as Bella B. reporting that Jewish students were required to attend chapel and sing Christian hymns in a Jewish hospital school and Ida I. as a

Jewish student wishing to join her colleagues in singing Christmas carols to patients and meeting hostility from a non-Jewish student.

No matter how these anti-Semitic incidents were generated or expressed, they were odious and destructive. They may or may not have succeeded in wounding their intended targets, but they certainly always diminished the perpetrators. An interesting point is that when anti-Semitism reared its ugly head in a group, people often extended a hand of friendship and support. For example:

- Lenore L., the Army nurse subjected to ethnic slurs by some of her colleagues, found others who were open and honest in their relationships who became friends,
- Ida I., the nursing student whose instructor unequivocally squelched the hostile anti-Semitism of a fellow student, found an admirable role model,
- Hannah H., having fled Nazism only to be greeted with blatant anti-Semitism by fellow students on her first day in nursing school, met other students with wholesome attitudes who provided a true basis for lifelong friendships.

All too often, however, Jewish nurses have stood alone in handling unpleasant anti-Semitic situations. The respondents delineated various strategies for reacting to such situations. A common observation was the satisfaction they felt when they spoke out and were assertive, see for example the narratives of Deborah D., Donna D., Edith E., and Rena R. Thelma T., in expressing regret that she had not been more confrontational, admitted that it might not have changed anything, but she would have felt better about it. To paraphrase Bonnie B., the best strategy to combat anti-Semitism comes from empowerment and from the realization that we don't have to take it.

Other respondents described their experiences with proactive strategies, such as Melanie M., the nursing instructor who promoted cultural awareness among her students; Amy A., who actively participated with her fellow students in a Christian-oriented school to teach them about her religious heritage; Rose R., the nurse who made a practice of announcing "right off the bat" that she is Jewish; Martha M., the nurse who with her coworkers formed a group that encouraged open exchanges of cultural experiences.

Finally, in addition to cataloguing experiences with anti-Semi-tism, a few women (e.g., Melanie M., Millie M., and Barbara B.) commented on what they labeled as "anti-nurse" sentiments in the Jewish community. This issue of Jewish acquaintances who "look down on Jewish nurses" and expressions of disdain for nursing encountered in upper-middle-class Jewish settings are attitudes that did not appear to be widespread but were expressed often enough to be a concern. Indeed, it emerged as just one more issue that Jewish nurses must cope with in seeking and finding fulfill-ment in their chosen career.

In coming to grips with these negative experiences, Sylvia S. had this to say, "If they did occur, my nature was to put them out of my mind, because I have had a wonderfully positive experience . . . choosing nursing was luck. I loved every minute of it." Thelma T. said, "I love nursing because I love people. . . . My patients and their loved ones have given me far more than I could ever give to them." And, finally, in the words of Frieda F., whose narrative appears in the next chapter, "I cannot imagine choosing another profession over nursing. I find it very rewarding."

References

Lane, I. J. L. (1992, January). Ida June 'Idie' Levin Lane '36 (Pin #193) autobiographical sketch. *University of Wisconsin (Madison) Nurses Alumni Organization Newsletter.*

Schorr, T. M., & Zimmerman, A. (1988). *Making choices, taking chances: Nurse leaders tell their stories.* St. Louis: Mosby.

9

As We See Ourselves:
"I Am A Nurse And Jewish.
The Two Have Been Very Interrelated in My Life"

In Chapter 8, the experiences of Jewish nurses were presented from the perspective of "as others see us." The focus of this chapter is on "as we see ourselves." Many Jewish women in nursing have faced the reality of upholding their values, customs, and traditions in a profession that is historically connected to Christianity. In addition, some have had to reconcile their commitment to nursing with negative attitudes among their own coreligionists. The women who responded to the survey offered some interesting insights into these and other concerns of Jewish nurses.

Many of the respondents who shared their stories discussed their family background in great detail. Most of them were born and raised in the United States. However, the immigrant experience figured prominently in the narratives of some of the women who recalled their origins just one or two generations away from the wretched ghettos of Eastern Europe. They described their life events within the context of their acculturation into American society and into the world of nursing. The respondents also spoke about the significance of Judaism in their lives, and they identified various ways in which they sought to fulfill their commitment to their religious tradition. In addition, some of them traced the link between their Jewish heritage and their choice of a nursing career in a largely Christian milieu. Finally, nearly all of the respondents spoke positively about their nursing experiences. As the stories that follow illustrate, the respondents are a diverse group of women influenced by their heritage and committed to their profession.

The Immigrant Experience.
"They Came to the United States and Became Proud Citizens."

The respondents in this category included a few women who

were immigrants to this country in the early years of the 20th century. Others were daughters and granddaughters of immigrants who had come earlier. Nearly all of the immigrants came from Eastern Europe, primarily from the territories that were part of czarist Russia, where they or their ancestors had endured a perilous existence under tyranny, experiencing persecution, poverty, and constant threats to their well-being. Their reactions to the "Golden Land" or, as they referred to it in Yiddish, *goldeneh medineh*, where they had come to enter society and to create a new life, are reflected in a variety of ways in the narratives of the respondents.

The first two stories are excerpts of narratives from respondents who came to this country as immigrants. Both Anna A. and Deena D. arrived in the early years of the 20th century. Deena, after many years, could still recall the frightening details of her family's flight from persecution. Both respondents spoke warmly about their careers in nursing.

Anna A. was one of 13 children born into a religious family in a small town in Poland in the early 1900s. Her father had a lumberyard, and he was a respected member of the community. Anna was 8 years old when World War I began, and the family had to abandon their home and business. They fled to Vienna where Anna attended school, learned German, and was tutored in English and Hebrew. When Anna was in her teens, she immigrated first to England and then to the United States to join her sisters who had arrived here earlier. Anna went to work making men's ties, then heard about a 9-month course in a Jewish maternity hospital. In addition to training, it offered lodging, kosher food, and a salary that enabled Anna to send money to help her family in Europe. Eventually, all but two family members were able to come to the United States. Anna completed the nursing course and in 1928, at the age of 22, received a certificate in obstetrical nursing from the Jewish Maternity Hospital in New York. She continued to work into the 1930s and, in 1941, received a license to practice as a practical nurse. In her later years, Anna talked about how she "missed being a nurse" and said she often dreamed about those days (Ruth Gutstein, daughter of Anna, personal communication, 1992, 1993, & 2000).

Deena D. was born into a religious Zionist family in Russia. Her father was active in the Herzl Zionist movement. Her maternal grandfather was a rabbi. "We experienced the pogroms, the Cossacks, and fleeing persecution was very frightening for a little girl like me." The Russian Revolution broke out in 1917 in the midst of their plans to emigrate, and it took them 5 years before they reached America. From the time that she entered nursing, Deena's motivation was fueled by her desire to care for the sick and to do good deeds. She had a rewarding career in nursing and even though she "retired" at age 62, she continued to take occasional postoperative cases for private duty. "Nursing was beneficial to me. I was able to be married and work at the same time, supporting my family during hard times." Her daughter is a nurse.

The next five narratives, from nurses who were daughters of immigrants, include moving statements about the immigrant experience. Louise L.'s story reflects the contempt her father felt for czarist rule and points to his success in establishing a family that was highly respected in his new country. Beth B. spoke about the financial hardships that her family endured. Adena A. referred to the values of social justice that were transmitted. The narratives of Bessie B. and Naomi N. embody their love for nursing. Bessie B.'s immigrant parents were proud of their daughter for having a career. Naomi N. spoke about her parents' joy in being citizens of a free country and about her strong commitment to Judaism.

Louise L. reported that her parents were immigrants from Eastern Europe who came to the United States before World War I. Her father left Russia at the age of 14, because he did not want to serve in the czar's army where Jewish soldiers were targets of official acts of bigotry. He worked and brought the rest of his family over. Louise grew up in a small town in a Mid-Atlantic state where there was a closely knit community of about 80 Jewish families who were highly respected by the community at large. Louise's family was very religious and she spoke Yiddish before she spoke English. She entered a Jewish hospital school of nursing in a major city, following her older sister, and had a long and rewarding career.

Beth B., in her early 70s, recalled growing up in a small New England city with a large Jewish community. She was one of four children, born to immigrant parents from Lithuania. Beth's parents were not well off financially. Her mother took in laundry and Beth helped her with it. There was no strong religious identity in the family—they did not celebrate Jewish holidays or observe the Sabbath. Beth had a remarkably successful career in nursing, earning national and international recognition.

Adena A. spoke about her maternal grandmother who immigrated to the United States from Russia at age 18 (with a 14-month-old child, Adena's mother) in the early 1900s and went to work in a sweatshop. Adena came from a home where Yiddish was spoken but where there were no rituals practiced, no synagogue affiliation, and no formal religious training. In her family, Judaism was expressed as "culture" or "tradition" rather than as "religion." Social justice was regarded as the cornerstone of Judaism, and, along with literary and political ideals, it was an important family value. "My grandmother always taught me that you give back to the community," she said. Adena's career in nursing was short, but she became a political activist and served effectively for many years in both elected and appointed public office positions, where she wielded influence concerning health issues and women's issues.

Bessie B. reported that her parents were immigrants from Lithuania and were proud of their daughter for having a career. She was raised in a fairly large city in the Midwest in an Orthodox Jewish home. Bessie said she worked as a nurse until the age of 70, and she would have gone on working but she suffered a broken hip and had to retire. At the time of her retirement, Bessie was working in a Roman Catholic hospital in a big city in one of the southern states. She loved nursing very much and still keeps up with the nursing journals.

Naomi N. wrote, "I am happy I became a nurse. Nursing is a career very much within the Jewish ethic of 'helping.' 'Helping professions' have been the professions of women of my day." Naomi said she was born and raised in a big city in a border state. "Both of my parents came to the United States in their teens and became proud citizens." Naomi came from a family with a strong, Jewish background and developed a lifelong commitment to Jewish learning and to Zionism. She is retired and speaks positively about her work as a school nurse.

The narratives in the next segment, like some others presented earlier, portray the economic hardships endured by immigrant families. Nonetheless, the following two respondents describe their parents' joy at being in this country, for, as both Rose R. and Bluma B. reported, their forebears had been through bloody pogroms and were thankful to have escaped to a new life in a free country. They also spoke about their families having lived in agricultural settlements established for Jewish immigrants. Now well advanced in years, these daughters of immigrants commented on their strong Jewish background and their success in nursing.

Bluma B., at age 102, recalled her origins as the child of Jewish immigrants who had fled Russia after a particularly bloody pogrom. She spoke about her father who, she said "was well-learned in

Jewish studies." She was born on a farm in Alliance, N.J., in 1888 and said Judaism was very important in her family's life. Her father was a leading member of one of the agricultural communities sponsored by the prominent Jewish philanthropists, Baron de Hirsch and Jacob Schiff, to encourage the settlement of Jewish immigrants away from large cities. From early childhood, she recalled the family "receiving well-dressed visitors who came to talk with Father and to inspect our farm. . . . Whenever 'Uncle Jacob' came to call, we . . . were particularly delighted, because . . . he always brought a whole chocolate bar for each of us" (Purmell, 1981). Uncle Jacob was, of course, Jacob Schiff, who, when he came to visit, used to bounce her on his knee. She reported that when she became a nurse, she "wrote an article for a nursing magazine on how to cope with fear; I conquered fear and wrote to my father about it." Bluma had a long and varied career in nursing and became the successful owner and administrator of a nursing home. In her 80s, after she retired, she began painting and produced fine works of art. In her 90s, she wrote and published her autobiography.

Rose R.'s parents were immigrants from Eastern Europe. She reported that her mother came from Rumania where she had lived close to a Romany (gypsy) community and "learned their ways." Her father's family had lived through very bad times—both of his parents were killed in a pogrom. Rose's parents were married in the United States in 1900. They lived in New Jersey in one of the agricultural communities funded by Baron de Hirsch. Eventually they made their home in a large urban area where they were very poor but had a supportive home life in a close-knit family. Rose recalled that, as a child, she went to a "Jewish school," learned "Jewish," had to sit through long *Sedarim* on Passover but did not go to synagogue. Her grandfather was a very religious man who often quoted from the *Torah*. Rose's mother served as the "neighborhood nurse" in an area populated mostly by Italian immigrants, who referred to her as "the Jew," but not in a derogatory way—they considered her to be a "healer." "My mother was a very pragmatic person, very down to earth; from her came my desire to be a nurse," said Rose. After Rose was discharged from World War II military service, she married and had a family. Judaism permeated her whole life as a daughter, mother, and nurse. In her later years, she owned and operated a nursing home for over three decades.

The next stories are about two women who surmounted difficulties as immigrants' offspring seeking to create their own roles in society. Ida I. had to overcome her parents' bias, which favored higher education for sons but not for daughters. Inherent in Ida's narrative is her love for nursing through which she found her place in life and was able to overcome her immigrant parents' objections. Pauline P. reported having had to deal with the snobbery of her Americanized Jewish family members toward her immigrant father. Pauline also spoke about her commitment to nursing and how she derived great satisfaction and self-respect at having achieved her goal despite negative family influences associated with her immigrant father's background.

Ida I. was the daughter of Russian Jewish immigrants who came to the United States in 1903 and 1904. She reported starting school in a one-room rural school house in the Midwest and later, through her own efforts, was the first Jewish student to enter the nursing school at a major state university in the 1930s. Her parents were supportive of her brothers' desire for higher education but believed that she, as a girl, did not need to go to college. Ida convinced her parents that university training and nursing went hand-in-hand to prepare her for a professional role, and she financed her own education. In nursing, Ida said that she had found her true calling and added, "I've loved every minute of my work . . . and learned to love people, all people. I feel I've made a positive difference in many people's lives and by doing so, gained a rewarding growing experience for myself."

Pauline P. reported that when she was only 3 years old, she lost her mother, who died at an early age. Pauline's father had come from Kiev when he was 15. He remarried when Pauline was 6 years old. His new wife was a young woman who, along with her family, took over the care of this little girl. The family members were third generation American Jews and could not understand why their daughter would marry "a greenhorn—a widower with a child and not even an American." Pauline recalled from her childhood how distressing it was to hear their critical references to the "differences between American Jews and East European Jews." Moreover, her immigrant father had not approved of her going into nursing. Nonetheless, Pauline was determined to overcome these difficulties. She gained a sense of satisfaction and self-respect by successfully meeting the challenges of her nursing school program and found fulfillment in her nursing career.

A new dimension was added to the immigrant experience in the aftermath of the Holocaust, which, along with World War II, was perpetrated by Nazi Germany. While this monumental tragedy of the 20th century touched the lives of Jewish people everywhere, its direst consequences were borne by the European Jews who were directly caught up in its vast horrendous machinery. One of the respondents identified herself as a Holocaust survivor, and several others described themselves as children of Holocaust survivors. Their families came to the United States where they found refuge in a free and open society. Here the respondents sought and achieved fulfillment in a rewarding career, as did Hannah H.

Hannah H. reported that in 1939 she and her family fled their native land after it was seized by the Nazis. When she came to the United States, she believed that going into nursing would put meaning into her life in the wake of the events in Europe. Hannah speaks of having a strong Jewish identity.

Emily E., Lorna L., and Francine F., who were children of Holocaust survivors, did not specifically connect that experience to their career in nursing, as Hannah H. did. Nonetheless, they spoke very positively about how they and their families felt toward nursing. For example, Emily E.'s parents were proud of her accomplishments, Lorna L. "loves" her work, and nursing is "a very important issue" for Francine F. All of these nurses spoke clearly about their commitment to nursing. Moreover, these three nurses, as did Hannah H., linked the Holocaust part of their family background with their Jewish experience and with their strong ties to Judaism.

The Jewish Experience—
"Judaism Is Very Important in My Life"

Many of the respondents discussed, with great feeling, their devotion to Judaism and to their Jewish heritage, which cut across the conventional branches of Judaism—Conservative, Orthodox, Reconstructionist, and Reform. They described their family backgrounds and their own efforts to create meaningful ways to live according to the Jewish tradition in a free and open society. They placed their adherence to the Judaic tradition in juxtaposition with their choice of nursing, which has often been characterized as a Christian profession. They mentioned specific Jewish communal organizations, societies, and institutions to which they had made commitments. They affirmed their connection and loyalty to Judaism even though it was not always through spiritual or religious bodies.

Respondents in the first segment of this group referred to their

Jewish background in terms of their roots. Their narratives, for the most part, reflect a positive commitment to their Jewish heritage, which they connected with the influence of their immigrant parents or grandparents. Several referred to the firmness of their convictions or to the confidence in their Jewish heritage and how this has helped them through difficult situations. They spoke about their commitment to observing religious practices and how they reconciled this with the requirements of their work schedules.

Bella B. recounted her early childhood growing up in a large city in the Midwest. Her parents, who were immigrants from Eastern Europe, raised the family in a traditional Jewish home. Bella reported having a productive and satisfying career and said, "I talked my sister into going into nursing." Her daughter also became a nurse.

Charlotte C., in her 70s, said that she came from a religious background and attended Hebrew school. Charlotte's father was an immigrant and her mother was born in the United States to immigrant parents. Charlotte knew Yiddish and often interpreted for patients who were Holocaust survivors.

Sylvia S., a national and international nursing leader, reported coming from a Jewish background, which she described as "mixed." Her parents were immigrants from Central and Eastern Europe. They observed the High Holidays and adhered to some customs and rituals in their home. Sylvia's grandmother and other members of the extended family were much more observant of the Orthodox Jewish tradition than were her parents. Nonetheless, Judaism was important in Sylvia's life. She and her parents maintained close ties and spent holidays with other members of the extended family.

Sandra S. wrote that she had a strong, well-informed Jewish background and was confident and comfortable in her role. Sandra earned her BSN as a second degree in a baccalaureate program in a university located in a small city in one of the Mid-Atlantic states, where not many Jewish people live. "Because I went . . . part-time, from 1975 to 1984, I was a member of several classes . . . there was never another Jewish person in any of my classes." As an Orthodox Jew, Sandra worked out a strategy with her instructors so that observing Jewish holidays was not a problem. She negotiated compromises in her assignments at the hospital when weekend work was required. At the hospital, Sandra often filled the role of consultant concerning Jewish rituals and dietary practices.

Nora N. also reported contributing her expertise to fellow staff members. "I came from a solid Jewish background . . . was educated in Yiddish in the Workmen's Circle schools . . . got religious training in Hebrew School," she said. At the Roman Catholic hospital where she worked, Nora sat on the ethics committee to present the Jewish point of view and was an interpreter for patients who spoke only Yiddish.

Evelyn E. recalled that her Jewish origins went back to a "relatively small town family life." She now has become very observant of Jewish traditions and schedules her work so that she is free on the Sabbath and on Jewish holidays. Negotiating these arrangements has not posed problems for Evelyn. "In fact," she says, "I find that there is more acceptance in the Christian community than in the Jewish community."

"Judaism was very much a part of our life when I was growing up," said Deborah D. Deborah's parents were very active in their synagogue, and she and her siblings attended Hebrew school. She continued this tradition in her own marriage and family life. Deborah said she felt very secure in her Jewish background, which has helped her through some uncomfortable situations.

Like Deborah D. in the previous segment, the nurses who provided narratives for the next segment spoke about their formative years, and they delineated the ways in which they established their commitment to their ethnic and religious heritage. Several of them also described how they carried over these religious activities into their adult lives.

Edith E. reported coming from a committed, traditional Jewish background. She went to Hebrew school and was active in the synagogue youth group. The lives of her family and friends were centered around the synagogue. "Judaism is very important in my life," she said. Edith completed a baccalaureate nursing program at a state university and, after graduation, worked in post-operative surgical nursing.

Leslie L. reported growing up in a big city in one of the southern states, where she presently works as a neonatal nurse. She came from a family with a strong Jewish background. As a youngster, Leslie participated in the Bnai Brith youth groups, went to Hebrew school, and was confirmed. She and her family were very active in the Jewish community. Leslie's mother and several of her aunts were nurses. Leslie is presently very involved in a leadership role in various Jewish communal affairs—her synagogue, the Hebrew Day School, and the Jewish community center.

Donna D. reported coming from a family where the commitment to Judaism was strong. "My religion has only helped me—never hurt me," she said. Donna holds a doctoral degree and is a highly respected nursing educator in a setting where she has succeeded in raising the consciousness of colleagues to the religious requirements and sensitivities of the students in her classes.

A few nurses commented on their frustration at not finding the degree of support or solidarity that they would have liked in order to fulfill their goal of observing Jewish practices within the framework of nursing. The next two narratives illustrate this point.

Gladys G. reported coming from a traditional Jewish background. She studied at a Jewish hospital nursing school where all except two of the students in her class were Jewish, but she noted that little emphasis was placed on Jewish identity or practices. After graduation, Gladys worked in a Jewish hospital in another city, where she felt more comfortable because greater attention was paid to Jewish tradition and rituals.

Susan S. wrote about having a strong Jewish identity and a firm commitment to traditional Jewish practices. She said, while still in nursing school where the dean of nursing was Jewish, "I felt that it was terrible that the three other Jewish students and I couldn't be excused [for the High Holidays]." Susan added that she would like to observe the Sabbath, but "being a new RN, single, and working in a hospital, it is hard to ask to be off every Friday evening and Saturday."

The following narratives are about several Jewish nurses who served in the military. Some of these women offered descriptions of military experiences that were intimately linked to their Jewish background. Others simply commented on the details of their Jewish heritage.

Bernice B., in her late 70s, recalled her experiences in the military in World War II. She served in Iran where she met Iranian Jews who welcomed her into their midst and treated her as a special person. "They called me Queen Esther," she said. Later as she was being reassigned to Europe, she felt apprehensive when she learned that she would be going to Germany. In Germany, she visited Dachau and was involved in the care of concentration camp victims who had been sent to her hospital at Reinau.

Lenore L. reported coming from an Orthodox Jewish family in a large city and studying at a Jewish hospital nursing school. Lenore grew up in a kosher home in a Jewish neighborhood. In 1945, she enlisted in the military and served in the Army Nurse Corps for nearly 2 years. At one point, Lenore was sent to a hospital in a major city in one of the southwestern states, where the Jewish community warmly received her and other Jewish military personnel in their homes and congregation. When she returned to civilian life, Lenore continued to enjoy a successful and rewarding career in school nursing.

Adele A., in her 70s, recounted her student years at a Jewish hospital school of nursing and her Army Nurse Corps service during World War II. "I was taught to honor my heritage," she said. Rachel R., who looked back on a rewarding career in the military, maintained firm ties with her Jewish heritage. Rachel participated in Jewish observances wherever possible, either on her base or in the surrounding community. She said, "Usually . . . I would try to get the Jewish holidays off and generally had no difficulty."

The remaining stories in this group include narratives from respondents who addressed the issue of their Jewish heritage in relation to their connection with Israel. The stories also show how some nurses reacted to the establishment of nurses councils in Hadassah.

Abby A. recalled growing up in a small town in a Mid-Atlantic state. She said her family was steeped in the modern-Orthodox Jewish way of life, where Jewish customs and rituals were upheld with respect and reverence. She studied nursing in the 1940s at a Jewish hospital school where the kosher tradition was observed. Abby has two daughters who live in Israel.

Ariela A., in her mid-30s, described herself as having a strong Jewish identity. She spoke reverently about the "nursing" tradition among her maternal forebears. Ariela said she especially likes working at the local Jewish hospital and enjoys "a special relationship with my Jewish patients . . . one of the most rewarding aspects of being a nurse." Ariela worked as a volunteer nurse in the Hadassah Hospital in Jerusalem and has welcomed the creation of the Hadassah Nurses Councils.

Millie M. expressed enthusiasm for the Hadassah Nurses Councils and has assumed a major leadership role in the organization.

Helen H. said she "grew up in a thoroughly American home and would describe myself and my family as 'gastronomically Jewish.'" Helen's family roots go back to Russia—her parents and one set of grandparents were born in the United States while the other grandparents came to the United States as young children. The family gathered on holidays, were affiliated with a synagogue, and she became involved with Bnai Brith, studied Hebrew in high school, and attended religious services with friends. After Helen completed nursing school, she went to Israel and worked at Hadassah hospital for 3 years and earned the Master of Public Health degree at Hebrew University. When Helen returned to this country, she worked at a children's hospital. She now has her own consulting practice for needs assessment, life-care planning, and legal consulting.

"Nursing is a Career Very Much Within the Jewish Ethic of Helping"

The final group of narratives is focused on the congruence of Judaism with nursing. In addition to expressing feelings about allegiance to their Judaic heritage and commitment to nursing, the nurses in this group trace a linkage between these two forces. In some of the examples, this linkage is implied, while in others it is uniquely and specifically stated. The respondents in this group came from a variety of Jewish backgrounds, and, like many of their colleagues, they spoke eloquently about their nursing careers.

In this first segment, the stories are by nurses who describe their experiences and imply a linkage between their Jewish heritage and their career in nursing.

Bertha B. wrote that "my career as a nurse was beneficial to me." Her mother was also a nurse. Bertha came from a family who practiced Conservative Judaism. She received religious training at home and in the synagogue where she attended religious school from the age of 6 to 16. Bertha, whose parents played an active role in their congregation, followed in their footsteps and has a sister who is a Reform rabbi.

Rhoda R. reported that observing holidays has always been important and that she has never had difficulty getting time off to attend services. "My religious beliefs were never kept secret, and I openly discussed our religious observance of holidays," she said. In Rhoda's career, she has derived great satisfaction in her relationships with her patients. "I think I played a positive role in the lives of many of my patients . . . I received much positive feedback along with much affection."

Alice A. recalled observing Jewish holidays, going to Hebrew School, and belonging to Bnai Brith Youth. She said their home was not kosher, but she now keeps a kosher home. She became a nurse-anesthetist and has made great strides in her field. Initially she had wanted to go into medicine but now says, "I am proud to say that I'm a nurse."

Fern F. explained that, although she was never part of a "practicing" Jewish family until about 10 years ago, she was always told that she was Jewish and she attended Sunday school for a while. She reported that "sometimes being Jewish feels strange to me since I don't feel that I have a lot of experience at it." Fern has tailored her employment so that she can spend more time at home with her children but added, "the longer I am away [from nursing] the more I seem to miss it." Fern's mother was also a nurse.

The narratives in the next segment are from respondents who spoke glowingly about their careers in nursing and implied a linkage of their commitment to Judaism with the satisfaction and rewards they have experienced in nursing.

Gloria G. reported having a firm Jewish identity. She said she grew up in a liberal Jewish background, in a Reform congregation, where she went to Hebrew school and was confirmed. Gloria studied basic nursing at a Jewish hospital school. "I never wanted anything but nursing; it has been a perfect career for me; I can make a living, and I feel I'm of help to someone else. At least once every day I've helped someone."

"Nursing has helped me find fulfillment as a human being," wrote Florence F., in her mid-60s. Florence said she had a rewarding career in public health nursing and in school nursing. Although she characterized her childhood family background as "sort of agnostic," she values her ties to the Judaic tradition, and she reached out with great interest for a connection with Jewish women in nursing.

When Bonnie B. was growing up, her family belonged to a Conservative Jewish congregation, but her parents were not involved in synagogue activities. Her family ties to Judaism were forged through the festivals. Bonnie reported that she did not go to Hebrew school, and the family was not too religiously observant. "My parents wanted to assimilate," she reported. However, being Jewish is important to Bonnie, who works at a Jewish hospital and believes that it is the best place to be. She said:

"Nursing offers in my professional life what I can be in my personal life; I look around and see homelessness, unwanted children, lack of access to health care, and nursing [at this Jewish hospital] addresses all of these things, takes care of all these problems."

Jane J. was born in the Midwest and raised in one of the southern states. Now in her mid-30s, Jane was the youngest of three children in a Conservative Jewish family where the Jewish tradition was important. She characterizes herself as a "caring, sensitive individual who has a desire to make people feel better." Jane said nursing was a natural choice. "My desire to help people has made me a better person." She reported that her nursing career has been a great benefit.

Annabelle A., now retired, wrote, "I am an Orthodox Jewish nurse." She described with great pride the superb education she received at the Jewish hospital school where she had studied many years ago. "I wish I could start all over again." Annabelle said she especially loved the hands-on aspect of providing patient care.

In the final segment of these narratives are reports from nurses who, from their experiences, have identified a unique and special bond between Judaic precepts and the practice of nursing.

Amy A. characterized her connection with nursing in terms of Judaic precepts, as a "personal need to help others . . . and a love for people." Amy's mother was also a nurse who "loved her profession." Amy and her mother participated in outreach and educational activities to demonstrate and interpret Jewish customs and rituals to non-Jewish colleagues in nursing.

Beverly B. said, "I was never very religious, though I came from an Orthodox Jewish family." The Jewish values with which Beverly identified were those related to education, intellectual pursuits, social justice, and performance of good work. She associates these values with nursing practice. As a young woman, Beverly reported being attracted to the Labor Zionist movement and went to Israel to work on a kibbutz. She admires those nursing leaders who espoused the goals and ideals of feminism and socialism, such as Lavinia Dock and Lillian Wald, and believes that Wald's drive for social change came out of the Jewish tradition. "Nursing is a wonderful career and I would recommend it to my children."

Gail G. identified strongly with the Judaic viewpoint inherent in the Talmudic teachings of "a well-known and great scholar who said that nurses are even more healing and more important than doctors when it comes to caring for the sick. The nurse gives the care and compassion that patients really need."

Frieda F. has been in nursing about 10 years. She specializes in oncology nursing. Frieda said:

[I encounter people every day who cannot believe]

that I could possibly be a nurse and Jewish as well. On the contrary, I believe the moral and ethical codes upon which the nursing profession is based are right in line with the Jewish religious beliefs . . . Judaism teaches us to be charitable and compassionate to our fellow man. I cannot imagine choosing another profession over nursing. I find it very rewarding.

Beatrice B. believes that "nursing is an altruistic profession; it appeals to Jewish morality . . . Jewish women have so much to contribute as caring people." In Beatrice's family, a strong Jewish consciousness with a real awareness and pride of being Jewish is evident. Beatrice holds a high executive position in nursing administration.

Brenda B. did not describe her family origins or Jewish background but noted that she places high value on learning and that "being Jewish only reinforces the knowledge that education is the key to life." And, in a brief but pungent statement, Maxine M. wrote, "I AM A NURSE AND AM JEWISH. THE TWO HAVE BEEN VERY INTERRELATED IN MY LIFE."

Summary

The foregoing accounts reflect on "as we see ourselves," and they incorporate a wide array of experiences of Jewish women in nursing. A recurrent theme among the respondents relates to the extent of their commitment to Judaism and its influence on their personal and professional lives. Some referred to their Jewish background in terms of being raised in a kosher home, observing the holidays, belonging to a synagogue, speaking Yiddish or hearing it spoken, going to Hebrew school, or connecting with Bnai Brith Youth or United Synagogue Youth (USY) groups. Among the older nurses there were references to attending Workmen's Circle schools. Some pointed out that they did not integrate any of these tangible practices into their lives, but they identified their Jewish commitment in terms of ideals and values that were transmitted by their parents and other family members as they were growing up—for example, social justice, intellectual pursuits, and performance of good deeds.

A young immigrant, Anna A., became a practical nurse, went to work, and earned enough money to enable her to help her family come to America. A Holocaust survivor, Hannah H., found renewed meaning and hope in life through nursing. The children of immigrants or Holocaust survivors or both, Emily E., Francine F., Lorna L., and others, were born into an open society where they sought and found fulfillment in a rewarding career.

Judging from the responses, we see ourselves as women, as members of the Jewish community, and as nurses in the larger world of nursing. We are mindful of our Jewish values and ideals as we juggle careers with our family lives. We are aware that some people in the non-Jewish community as well as in the Jewish community may harbor negative views about us as Jews, as nurses, and as Jewish women in nursing. Nevertheless, we:

- have been taught to honor our heritage;
- find that the moral and ethical codes upon which the nursing profession is based are in line with the Jewish religious beliefs;
- identify strongly with the Talmudic viewpoint that nurses may be even more healing and more important than are physicians when it comes to caring for the sick;
- believe that Judaism teaches us to be charitable and compassionate and that nursing is a career very much within the Jewish ethic of helping;
- consider that Lillian Wald's drive for social change came out of the Jewish tradition;
- believe that nursing is an altruistic profession, that it appeals to Jewish morality, and that Jewish women have much to contribute as caring people;
- recognize that being Jewish reinforces the knowledge that education is the key to life;
- cannot imagine choosing another profession over nursing;
- consider nursing to be a wonderful, rewarding career that we can recommend to our children;
- realize that nursing offers in our professional lives what we can be in our personal lives.

In the words of Maxine M., one of the respondents, "I am a nurse and Jewish—the two have been very interrelated in my life." This is "AS WE SEE OURSELVES."

References

Purmell, B. B. R. (1981). *A farmer's daughter: Bluma.* Los Angeles: Hayvenhurst Publishers.

10

**An Idea Whose Time Has Come:
The Hadassah Nurses Councils**

Origins

*B*adassah Nurses Councils? Where did the idea for their formation originate? It began in 1989 with two enterprising
Jewish women from the Boston area, Nancy Falchuk and Rachel
Albert. One (Falchuk) was a nurse, the other (Albert) was a strong
advocate of the nursing profession, and both were dedicated to
the Zionist ideals of Hadassah (the Women's Zionist Organization
of America). They were especially committed to that sphere of
Hadassah that provides a variety of hospital, medical, and health
services in Israel, the so-called HMO or Hadassah Medical Organization. One day it became clear to these women that nurses in
Israel were not being sufficiently recognized or nurtured.

The realization had dawned. Hadassah, after all, is essentially
a Jewish women's organization. Nursing is a profession largely
made up of women, where Jewish women are in the minority. It
was the pioneer effort of two American-Jewish nurses in 1913 that
paved the way for the vast network of services currently supported
in Israel by Hadassah. The time had come for Hadassah to reflect
on its roots and to turn its attention, once again, to nursing and
to nurses—that cadre of health workers who are the mainstay in
all health care delivery systems for the provision of health care
services.

From the Boston area, Albert and Falchuk gathered several like-
minded nurses who met in the spring of 1989 to discuss ways
of supporting the nursing staff at Hadassah's hospitals in Israel.
Nurses, as a rule, are cognizant of the fact that, within the overall
framework of society, their profession has often been altogether
overlooked or, at best, subsumed under the general heading of
"medical organization." Among Jewish nurses, in particular, there
is a perception that, within the Jewish community, in the state of
Israel and worldwide, their profession does not have a status equal
to that of other professions. The airing of Falchuk and Albert's

concerns was very well-timed. It struck a responsive chord within the ranks of Jewish nurses, who, by 1990, had begun to show signs of overcoming an innate reticence to make their presence known in the nursing profession. For example, in the summer of 1985, over 200 Jewish nurses in the greater Boston area had responded to a call by Dr. Rachel Spector to establish a networking group. Thus a nucleus for the first Hadassah nurses council had been pulled together through the efforts of Dr. Spector, who is known for her pioneering work in cultural diversity.

The National Center for Nurses Councils of Hadassah

In the spring of 1990, Falchuk and Albert went to the National Board of Hadassah with their idea of forming a national coalition of nurses committed to the ideals of Zionism and interested in networking with other Jewish colleagues in nursing. In June 1990, the Board voted to create a new department, the National Center for Nurses Councils of Hadassah. Up until that time, there was no other national organization for Jewish nurses. It must be noted, however, that there was a regional association, which had been formed several years earlier by a group of Jewish nurses in Connecticut. Known as the Association of Jewish Registered Nurses, they were very proud of their organization. They met regularly with interesting program offerings, and they raised money to provide scholarship assistance to nurses.

One of the first items on the agenda of the National Center for Nurses Councils was to increase its visibility by sponsoring a booth in the Exhibit Hall of the American Nurses' Association Convention held in the summer of 1990 in Boston. Hadassah was uniquely showcased in a setting that afforded a golden opportunity to inform and educate other nurses about the organization's goals and accomplishments. The members of the national center reported that their experience at the convention was refreshing and rewarding. Nurses from all walks of life greeted them enthusiastically, and Jewish nurses from every part of the country reiterated, "finally there is a place for us" (Volunteers Needed. ANA Convention, 1992, p. 2).

The success of this venture led to the center's support for a similar display, on a smaller scale, by the Philadelphia Council at the Pennsylvania Nurses Association Convention in 1991, where many nurses visited the exhibit to learn about Hadassah. The national center announced plans for having a booth at the 1992

American Nurses' Association Convention in Las Vegas (Volunteers Needed at ANA Convention, 1991). In 1993, Hadassah featured a creative entry, "Hadassah and the Nursing Connection: From the Past to the Future," at the Poster Session of the National League for Nursing Convention in Boston, which drew comments from many interested nurses who were in attendance.

Meanwhile, the Boston area nurses received their charter as the first Hadassah nurses group in the United States. One of the members expressed her sentiment about the group as follows:

> The Nurses Council has allowed me to put together two very important facets of my life and I can't begin to describe how wonderful it feels to be among women who understand what it is to be a nurse and to be Jewish. Alone no more! I never really thought about how I felt being a Jewish nurse until this group formed (Survey respondent, "Ariela A.").

The Boston group was named the Landy-Kaplan Nurses Council in honor of Rachel (Rae) Landy and Rose Kaplan, the two American nurses who were sent to Palestine by Henrietta Szold in 1913. At the inspiring charter ceremony, on April 24, 1990, Marlene Post, a nurse who served on the Hadassah National Board, addressed the group. She later became Hadassah's 21st national president. Among the guests, in addition to two prominent nursing leaders, Dr. Joyce Clifford and Dr. Anne Kibrick, were Edna Goldsmith (a cousin of Rachel Landy) and Judith B. Swartz, who was a generous benefactor for a Hadassah Nursing Exchange Program (First Hadassah Nurses Council Is Chartered, 1990). By the spring of 1991 two more local councils were officially chartered (Cleveland and Miami), and in that same year the national center was able to account for the formation of nurses councils in 20 other areas of the United States (News From the National Center for Nurses Councils, 1991).

Goals and Programs of the Nurses Councils

In November 1990, the national center organized and conducted the first Hadassah Nurses Mission to Israel, which led to a bond between Israeli and American nurses. Successive nurses' missions to Israel followed over several years—March 1992, February/ March 1993, February/March 1994. A feature of the March 1995 mission was the first joint nurses and social workers' meeting, and in March 1998 a nurses' mission was an integral part of the Hadassah Purim Miracle Mission to Israel. In May 2000, the 10th anniversary of the creation of the Nurses Councils, the nurses' tour to Israel included an outreach visit to nurses in Jordan.

In 1990-1991, the national center officials moved quickly to appoint an advisory board, which was made up of American leaders in nursing, and at their first meeting on December 15, 1991, they formalized a Statement of Purpose for the nurses councils as follows:

> Hadassah Nurses Councils are formed to:
> 1. establish an international partnership with the Nursing Division of the Hadassah Medical Organization in Jerusalem in order to enhance and support our profession in Israel and in the United States, and
> 2. meet the special educational, social, and professional concerns of Jewish and Zionist nurses in the United States and in Israel (Statement of Purpose, 1991).

At their first meeting, the members of the National Advisory Board also voted to create a special award—the Kaplan-Landy Award—to be presented at the Hadassah National Convention to an outstanding American Jewish nurse who "demonstrated vision, innovation, leadership, and caring within the profession and the community" (A Special Award For an Outstanding Jewish Nurse, 1992, p. 1). The first recipient of this award was Thelma Schorr, who was selected from a pool of highly illustrious and eminently qualified nominees. Schorr was honored at the Hadassah Convention in Washington, D.C., in 1992. In the next few years, this honor was awarded at Hadassah National Conventions to the following distinguished nurses: Dr. Claire Fagin, 1994 in New York; Dr. Anne Kibrick, 1995 in Israel (Chana Kurtzman, an Israeli nurse, was also honored in 1995); Dr. Ingeborg Mauksch, 1997 in Chicago; Dr. Barbara Heller, 1999 in Washington, D.C. No award was given in 2000, and in 2001 the award went to Dr. Nurit Wagner in Jerusalem.

The National Center launched the publication of a newsletter, *Nursing: The Jewish Connection*, which is edited by Thelma

Schorr and is issued about twice a year. Volume one, number one appeared in September 1990, and reports of activities from local councils were submitted. For the members of the councils, these reports reflected a commitment to their profession, a devotion to Judaism and to Zionism, a dedication to community service, and a desire for learning. Their programs were made up of a broad range of subjects, which included:

1. Jewish themes and issues, for example, Jewish Medical Ethics, Wisdom from the Jewish Tradition in Health and Healing, Anti-Semitism, and so on;
2. Women's special interest topics, for example, Women's Health Care, Domestic Violence, Women in the *Torah*, Women in the Work Force, and so on;
3. Nursing practice and nursing issues, for example, Changing Role of Nursing and the Nurse Practice Act, Nurse Empowerment, Transcultural Nursing, History of Nursing from the Jewish Perspective, and so on;
4. Medical topics, for example, Metabolic-Genetic Diseases, AIDS, Bone Marrow Transplants, Handling Biohazardous Materials, and so on;
5. Special ties with Israel, for example, Nursing and Nursing Education in Israel, the Hadassah Program in Israel, Relations between Israelis and American Jews, and so on.

These are but a few of the numerous and diverse program offerings, many of which awarded Continuing Education Units (CEUs) to members who attended. Reports sent to the newsletter described how various groups had devised innovative methods for networking, socializing, and raising funds to support nursing in Israel. The reports also included information about local councils that created prayer-in-health cards, offered health teaching programs, ran health fairs, and engaged in activities relevant to the Jewish community. For example, on the 50th anniversary of the end of World War II, one local council held a special program to honor Jewish nurses and other Jewish women who had served their country (On 50th Anniversary of End of World War II, 1996).

National Center for Nurses Councils Leadership

The first two leaders of the National Center for Nurses Councils were the cofounders—Rachel Albert and Nancy Falchuk. Through their creative leadership, the number of local councils continued to increase. They personally met with women at the grass roots level to inspire and to nurture the growth of the fledgling councils. They provided an opportunity for members to air their professional concerns and to express their goals and expectations.

From the beginning, Falchuk and Albert realized that many members of local councils viewed their role vis-a-vis Hadassah somewhat differently from the perceived role of many Hadassah members, who traditionally focus on fund raising. For example, in a needs assessment survey conducted by one of the local councils, respondents reported a high level of interest in networking and educational activities and a low level of interest in fund raising (Needs Assessment Survey, 1991). A common characteristic among the ranks was a conviction that Hadassah, as a Jewish women's organization, should be encouraged to strengthen its commitment to the support of nursing in Israel and to respond to the special needs of Jewish nurses in the United States. Falchuk and Albert, in collaboration with the national advisory board, worked tirelessly to address these needs.

By their example, Falchuk and Albert encouraged other capable women to come forth and fill the office of cochair, which has been held successively by Judy Garner, Janice Greenwald (RN), Marilyn Myers (RN), Ruth Grossberg, and Barbara Sabin (RN). Under the wise leadership of these dedicated women, the National Center for Nurses Councils can point with pride to accomplishments other than those already cited. For example, the national center conducted leadership training institutes for officers and members of local councils in 1996 and 1998 (Nurses Councils Report Activities at Leadership Training Institute, 1997; Leadership Training Institute Held in New York City, 1999). In addition, the national center has sponsored on several occasions a "Day on the Hill" program as an educational experience for council members. Those who enrolled went to Washington, D.C., and met with Israeli Embassy staff, with State Department officers, and with their own Congressional representatives. All who participated welcomed this enriching and rewarding experience.

Early Achievements

Perhaps the two most significant and dramatic achievements in the first decade of the National Center for Nurses Councils were the launching of a major relief mission to Bosnia and the forging of a collaborative arrangement for establishing a clinical master's in nursing (MSN) program in Israel.

Bosnian Relief Mission

In her adaptation of the Judaic precept that "whoever saves a single life is as if one saves the entire world," Elsie Roth, a Jewish nurse from the St. Louis area, wanted to take action after watching the nightly television reports of the ghastly scenes from the civil war raging in Bosnia. She urged Hadassah, through the National Center for Nurses Councils, to lend support to the organization of a relief mission to the beleaguered city of Sarajevo, the capital of Bosnia-Hercegovina. This was not Roth's first humanitarian project. In 1986, she went to the aid of Jews who were living in dire straits in northern Ethiopia. In 1991, she was a volunteer at a hospital trauma center in Tel-Aviv during Iraq's scud-missile attacks on Israel (Bosnian Serbs Reject Peace Plan, 1994). This time Elsie Roth persuaded Hadassah to stand behind her plan, which called for a fact-finding tour to Bosnia by a group of nurses to be followed by a delivery of needed supplies.

Roth and three other members of local nurses councils—Kathryn Bauschard from St. Louis, Mo., Deanna Pearlmutter from Boston, and Charlotte Franklin from Santa Barbara, Calif.—traveled in August 1994 to the war-torn region in the Balkans to assess local needs for pharmaceuticals and other medical supplies and equipment. They found the most deplorable conditions, and, above all, they heard expressions of helplessness and despair from the victims who had seen other visitors come to "assess" without any follow-up. When the team of nurses came back to the United States, a vigorous campaign was launched by Hadassah to collect the needed supplies.

By this time, Hadassah had connected with a key volunteer worker, Sherry Hahn, from a Boston-area Jewish group involved in humanitarian efforts for Bosnia. Hahn, through her organization, had already established contact with a highly respected voluntary service agency in the Jewish community of Bosnia—La Benevolencija—which would play a major role in handling and distributing the donations from Hadassah. Within 6 months, after 33 tons of medical supplies and clothing valued at $3.5 million were gathered, these materials were delivered to Sarajevo early in 1995. The shipment was accompanied by Roth, for Hadassah, and by Hahn, who coordinated the efforts through *La Benevolencija* in Bosnia (From Your National Office, 1995). A second campaign was launched, and within a year 75 tons of relief supplies, at an estimated value of over $10 million, were collected. Early in 1996, Hahn, Roth, and a Bosnian nurse living in St. Louis accompanied the shipment to Sarajevo for distribution by *La Benevolencija* (Hadassah Nurses Council Fulfills a Second Promise, 1996).

Janice Apple Malett, a member of the Lillian Wald Chapter of the Hadassah Nurses Council, expressed her gratitude to Hadassah for providing an opportunity to participate in this campaign and to Elsie Roth and Sherry Hahn for spearheading the effort. Malett mobilized her colleagues in the Wound/Ostomy/Continence (WOC) network to collect special supplies and equipment valued at $300,000. In an interview for the national council Newsletter, Malett said that as a Jewish nurse, she believed she had a unique part to play in this effort, because "growing up in the shadow of the Holocaust, I had constant questions about the role of the people in the Jewish community" (One Nurse's Response, 1996, p. 5). She added that her interest in Hadassah increased because of the nurses councils and that the Bosnia drive was "our most magnificent moment" (p. 5).

The Clinical Master's Program in Israel

Over the years, nurses in Israel have worked diligently to strengthen their nursing education programs, and Hadassah has played a role in these efforts. Hadassah's pioneer nursing education program began in Jerusalem with the establishment of the Hadassah School of Nursing in 1918, which graduated its first class in 1921 (Bartal & Steiner-Freud, 1999). In 1936, in honor of Henrietta Szold's 75th birthday, the school was renamed the Henrietta Szold Hadassah School of Nursing. Hadassah's nursing projects in the early 20th century became a model for neighboring areas such as Transjordan, Egypt, and the Isle of Rhodes (Benson, 1990a).

An attempt was made to transform the Henrietta Szold Hadassah School of Nursing into a university school in 1947 and again in 1953 (Stockler, 1988). Serious efforts to create a baccalaureate program got under way in the early 1970s when Dr. Anne Kibrick, a distinguished professor of nursing from Boston, was invited to Israel as a consultant to the Henrietta Szold Hadassah School of Nursing for the purpose of establishing a Bachelor of Science in Nursing (BSN) program (From Diploma to . . ., 1993). The process was long and involved, but in 1975 a generic BSN program was launched, the first of its kind in Israel, and the school was known as the Henrietta Szold Hadassah-Hebrew University School of Nursing.

More recently, at the instigation of the Hadassah National Center for Nurses Councils, nurses from the United States and from Israel entered into a collaborative relationship to initiate an Advanced Practice Clinical Master's Program in Israel. To represent the American team, Hadassah and the University of Maryland School of Nursing formed a partnership, which was announced by Marlene Post, national president of Hadassah, at a news conference in Baltimore on September 22, 1997. In Israel, the project was spearheaded by the director and faculty of the Jerusalem-based nursing school (Hadassah and Maryland School Celebrate Advanced Practice Clinical Master's Program, 1997).

Leading the overall collaborative arrangement for the clinical master's program are Marlene Post; Dr. Barbara Heller, dean of the School of Nursing at the University of Maryland; and Dr. Miri Rom, director and acting associate dean of the Henrietta Szold Hadassah-Hebrew University School of Nursing in Jerusalem. As the history of this program unfolds, its development has come to be regarded as one "of woman power and more specifically nurse power" (Update on Hadassah's Clinical Master's, 1998, p. 2).

Summary

This brief historical overview of the first decade of the Hadassah Nurses Councils attests to the courage, wisdom, and steadfastness of the women who have guided the course of this new endeavor. Nurses council members, so far, can point with pride to the significant achievements of the first 10 years. They have overcome hurdles and are ready to meet new challenges that lie ahead. With the establishment of the National Center for Nurses Councils and the formation of local nurses councils, Hadassah has broadened the horizons for Jewish nurses and for all nurses who are committed to Israel and to Zionism. "An idea whose time has come—at last we have the opportunity to join together as Jews, as women, and as nurses" (Benson, 1990b, p. 2).

References

Bartal, N., & Steiner-Freud, J. (1999). *The first graduating class: Hadassah School of Nursing 1921.* New York, NY: Hadassah, The Women's Zionist Organization of America.

Benson, E. R. (1990a, Spring). Hadassah and the nursing connection: Early days. *Bulletin of the American Association for the History of Nursing, 26,* 4-6.

Benson, E. R. (1990b, September). Nursing and the Jewish connection. In *Nursing: The Jewish connection.* Hadassah National Center for Nurses Councils Newsletter, p. 2.

Bosnian Serbs reject peace plan. (1994, August 30). *St. Louis Post Dispatch,* pp. 1, 6.

First Hadassah nurses council is chartered! (1990, June). *Landy-Kaplan Nurses Council, Boston Chapter of Hadassah Newsletter,* pp. 1, 4.

From diploma to . . . (1993, Fall). *Nursing: The Jewish Connection.* Hadassah National Center for Nurses Councils Newsletter, p. 6.

From your national office. (1995, Spring/Summer). *Nursing: The Jewish Connection.* Hadassah National Center for Nurses Councils Newsletter, p. 1.

Hadassah and Maryland school celebrate advanced practice clinical master's program. (1997, Fall/Winter). *Nursing: The Jewish Connection.* Hadassah National Center for Nurses Councils Newsletter, pp. 1, 3.

Hadassah nurses council fulfills a second promise. (1996, Spring). Nursing: *The Jewish Connection.* Hadassah National Center for Nurses Councils Newsletter, p. 12.

Leadership training institute held in New York City. (1999, Spring/Summer). *Nursing: The Jewish Connection.* Hadassah National Center for Nurses Councils Newsletter, p. 6.

Needs assessment survey. (1991). Philadelphia Chapter of Hadassah Nurses Council (unpublished).

News from the National Center for Nurses Councils. (1991, April). *Nursing: The Jewish Connection.* Hadassah National Center for Nurses Councils Newsletter, p. 2.

Nurses councils report activities at leadership training institute. (1997, Spring/Summer). *Nursing: The Jewish Connection.* Hadassah National Center for Nurses Councils Newsletter, p. 6.

One nurse's response. (1996, Spring). *Nursing: The Jewish Connection.* Hadassah National Center for Nurses Councils Newsletter, p. 5.

On 50th anniversary of end of World War II . . . (1996, Spring). *Nursing: The Jewish Connection.* Hadassah National Center for Nurses Councils Newsletter, p. 10.

A special award for an outstanding Jewish nurse. (1992, February). *Nursing: The Jewish Connection.* Hadassah National Center for Nurses Councils Newsletter, p. 1.

Statement of purpose. (1991, September). *Nursing: The Jewish Connection.* Hadassah National Center for Nurses Councils Newsletter, p. 2.

Stockler, R. A. (1988). *Two decades of academic education for nurses—Tel-Aviv University (p. 9).* Tel-Aviv, Israel: Department of Nursing, Sackler Faculty of Medicine.

Update on Hadassah's clinical master's. (1998, Spring/Summer). *Nursing: The Jewish Connection.* Hadassah National Center for Nurses Councils Newsletter, p. 2.

Volunteers needed. ANA convention. (1992, February). *Nursing: The Jewish Connection.* Hadassah National Center for Nurses Councils Newsletter, pp. 1, 2.

Volunteers needed at ANA convention. (1991, September). *Nursing: The Jewish Connection.* Hadassah National Center for Nurses Councils Newsletter, p. 2

Milestones*
Development of The Hadassah School of Nursing

JERUSALEM: 1918-1988

1918 School of Nursing founded by Hadassah

1921 First class of 22 nurses graduated

1923 First post basic course established—public health nursing

1936 Henrietta Szold's 75th birthday—school renamed "Henrietta Szold Hadassah School of Nursing"

1939 School moved to its new building on Mount Scopus

1939-45 Students and graduates contributed to WWII effort; school expanded; developed postgraduate courses in operating room, public health, and midwifery

1945-47 Students and graduates participated in struggle for independence; graduates volunteer in displaced person camps in Germany and detainee camps on Cyprus

1948 Ambush of Hadassah convoy; school left Mt. Scopus on May 11, moved to temporary quarters in the St. Joseph's convent; War of Independence—Siege of Jerusalem; half of graduates drafted into Israel Defense Forces

1949 Courses for auxiliary personnel (including LPNs) opened by Hadassah in Jerusalem and Beer-Sheva

1953 Curriculum revised; integration of family and community health nursing in basic curriculum; first steps taken in preparation for university education of nurses

1960 Education of nurses from developing countries begun as a joint project with the Department of International Cooperation of the Foreign Ministry of Israel

1961 School moved to its new building at the Medical Center Kiryat Hadassah, Ein Kerem

1968 Henrietta Szold prize to the nurses of Hadassah awarded by Hadassah on the 50th anniversary of the school

1970	Decision reached to open the first generic baccalaureate program for nurses in Israel
1972	Four nurse teachers sent to United States to study clinical nursing at graduate and postgraduate levels
1974	First upgrading course for feldshers from Russia established
1975	The four-year generic baccalaureate nursing program opened within the framework of Hebrew University; upgrade course for LPNs established
1979	First class graduated from the baccalaureate program
1981	Assaf-Harofe School of Nursing affiliated with Henrietta Szold Hadassah Hebrew University School of Nursing; 3-year diploma program phased out
1982	Baccalaureate completion program for RNs established; first post basic course for RNs in intensive care opened; Jerusalem municipality awarded Henrietta Szold prize to the school of nursing during Hadassah's 70th anniversary celebration
1984	Kaplan School of Nursing affiliated with Henrietta Szold Hadassah-Hebrew University School of Nursing
1985	Student exchange program with University of Pennsylvania School of Nursing established
1986	Course offering career change option for university graduates in fields other than nursing established
1987	Judith Steiner-Freud, class of 1944 and former director of the school, awarded the distinguished graduate award by Hadassah at its 75th anniversary convention
1988	School celebrated its 70th anniversary with hundreds of graduates participating

*Adapted from a report by Chana Kurtzman, director of the school of nursing and associate dean, and by Judith Steiner-Freud.

Part III

Lest We Forget

11

✡ Jewish Nurses in Wartime Service

A careful reading of nursing history shows nursing in apposition to the military and elicits the point that "nursing has made its greatest advances and notable achievements in connection with wars" (Donahue, 1985, p. 394). From time immemorial men waged wars, endlessly fighting, killing, wounding, maiming, and leaving in their wake death, disease, and disruption in the lives of millions of innocent people. In times of war, women emerged from their homes and families and went out to nurse the sick and wounded, and comfort those who were suffering. This theme has been dramatized and immortalized in works of art and literature on legendary and reality-based events (Benson, 1991; Dolan, 1978). The early 20th century Swedish feminist-pacifist writer, Ellen Key, epitomizes this theme in her classic monograph, *Florence Nightingale and Bertha von Suttner: Two Women at War Against War* (Key, 1919; Benson, 1984). In this work, Key praises the humanitarianism of Florence Nightingale as a nurse who went out to alleviate human suffering brought on by war. Key contrasts Nightingale's role with the pacifist mission of Baroness Bertha von Suttner, who strove to prevent the outbreak of war.

The women who came forth, throughout history, to offer their services during wartime have been singled out for special recognition by nurse historians. For example, in Chapter 3 reference is made to the characterization of 19th century wartime volunteer "nurses" as prototypes in the development of the modern, secular profession of nursing. Indeed, the wartime service of women has figured so prominently in the annals of nursing history that the time has come, lest we forget, to identify the role of Jewish women in these endeavors. The text documents the fact that in the early 19th century Jewish women were among the ranks of volunteers who patriotically answered the call for nurses in times of war and other national emergencies. For instance, we noted Rahel Varnhagen's work during the Napoleonic wars as well as the contribution of other German-Jewish women in later 19th century skirmishes (Kaplan, 1991). To add to the story, let us now look for other examples of the presence of Jewish women in 19th and 20th century wartime service with regard to this singular dimension of nursing history.

Pre-World War I

The Crimean War in the 1850s was the "launching pad" for Florence Nightingale in her mission to refashion nursing as it existed at that time. The nurses who served under Nightingale included Roman Catholic nursing sisters, Anglican nursing sisters, and other nurses not connected with religious orders (Donahue, 1985). On the other side of the battle, Russian women, most of whom had had no hospital experience or training, had been recruited and organized by the Grand Duchess Elena Pavlovna of the Imperial Russian Court to serve in the Crimea as a semi-religious group of volunteer nurses (Benson, 1992). There are no historic references to the participation of Jewish women on either side of this battle except for a brief mention, almost in passing, of one Lola Magnus, who was "born in Odessa and served as a nurse in the Crimean War" (Chernow, 1993, p. 73).

In the United States, the Civil War accentuated the need for nurses in wartime. It has already been noted that Jewish women in the North and South answered the call for volunteer nurses in the Civil War and that they participated actively in organizing and providing care for military casualties. Indeed, the role played by women in that conflict not only paved the way for the development of modern, secular nursing in America but also served as a model for providing care when war broke out between the United States and Spain at the end of the 19th century.

During the Spanish-American War, the Surgeon General at first thought that no help was needed for the Hospital Corps, but when conditions grew worse he issued a call for women to serve as nurses. The first contingent of graduate nurses to serve in the United States Army signed on for service in May 1898, and within a few months over 1,100 nurses were added to the group. Other persons were recruited including Native American women, African American women, nuns from religious orders, and some men (Sarnecky, 1997). No reference is made to the presence of Jewish women. However, it has been noted that Rose Kaplan was a nurse in the Spanish-American War (see Chapter 5).

In the years leading up to World War I, the Balkan Wars of

1912-1913, with their bloody battles, disrupted the lives of millions of people in that part of the world (Benson, 1974). Women in Serbia responded patriotically to the call for help, and among their ranks was a Jewish woman, Nettie Munk (1864-1924), who distinguished herself as a volunteer nurse during the Balkan Wars and during World War I. In cooperation with the Serbian Red Cross, Munk set up temporary hospitals near the battlefront. She organized care for the sick and wounded, raised funds, and gathered relief supplies and equipment. Munk earned the gratitude of her fellow citizens, who hailed her as a great humanitarian (Natalija - Neti Munk, 1974; Rene Gremaux, personal communication, June 2000).

World War I

The troubled events in the Balkans were exacerbated when, on June 28, 1914, a member of the Young Bosnia Society assassinated the Austrian Archduke and his wife, who were on a special visit to Sarajevo. The Great Powers of Europe used this incident to trigger the onset of World War I in 1914. The United States entered the war nearly 3 years later in April 1917. In June 1917, the Committee on Nursing of the General Medical Board of the United States Council of National Defense was officially sanctioned by President Woodrow Wilson (Sarnecky, 1999). The committee, headed by Adelaide Nutting, faced the challenge of evaluating and mobilizing the nursing resources that were required for the military. The American Red Cross was also involved, and 6 months after America entered the war, nearly 1,100 nurses had gone overseas (Kalisch & Kalisch, 1986).

During World War I, over 21,000 women served with the American Army as nurses, of whom nearly one-half were sent to France (Sarnecky, 1999). Although no documentation of numbers is available, Jewish nurses were among those who served on the home front and in Europe. See, for example, Amelia Greenwald (Chapter 5) and Rae Landy (Chapter 5). Both Greenwald and Landy served with American forces throughout the war. After the war, Landy stayed on in the military through World War II. Among the other Jewish nurses cited in Chapter 5, it is interesting to note that Naomi Deutsch was a member of the American Red Cross and tried to enlist in the armed forces in World War I. The military refused to accept her because of "her place of birth"; she was born in the city of Brno in Moravia, which at that time was part of the Austro-Hungarian empire (Mayer, 1997). In World War I, Regina Kaplan also attempted to enlist, but was rejected because of her height, and Mathilda Scheuer was turned down because of "an impacted tooth" (Biographical Notes on Mathilda Scheuer, 1960).

The full extent of the participation of Jewish nurses in World War I is a part of history that has not been fully explored. The 1999 exhibit of *Women in the Military: A Jewish Perspective* by the National Museum of American Jewish Military History showed a brief sketch of a Jewish woman, Ethel Gladstone, who was born and raised in Chicago and became a registered nurse after completing her program at West Side Hospital. Gladstone enlisted for service in March 1918 and went overseas with the Fifth Army Corps Expeditionary Force. She was on active duty until the end of the war in November 1918, and then she continued to serve with the Army in Germany until July 1919 (Women in the Military, 1999).

On the other side of the battle in World War I, Jewish women in Germany performed their patriotic duty for their country as nurses in wartime. The Frankfurt Society of Jewish nurses turned its dormitory over for use as an army infirmary (Kaplan, 1991). Jewish women volunteered through the German Red Cross, the National Women's Service, and various Jewish women's groups. They served at the front where they functioned as "nurses" (Kaplan, 1991). Resi Weglein, a Jewish nurse who lived through World War II and survived internment at Theresienstadt, had served in World War I as a Red Cross volunteer nurse (Benson, 1995). Another German-Jewish nurse, Schwester Selma Maier, who died in 1984 in Israel at the age of 100, was sent to Palestine from Germany to fulfill her obligation for wartime service during World War I. At that time, Turkey ruled Palestine and was an ally of Germany (Benson, 1995).

The Spanish Civil War

The Spanish Civil War in the 1930s galvanized hundreds of idealistic young Americans and other foreign nationals into action. They viewed this conflict as a struggle between the evil forces of Fascism and the democratically established Second Republic of Spain. This conflagration lasted for 3 years and turned into a testing ground for World War II. Italy's Mussolini and Germany's Hitler bolstered the Fascist dictator, Generalissimo Franco, while the world's democracies remained neutral and did not come to the aid of the legally constituted Spanish government. Individual nurses from the United States and from many other countries around the world went to Spain and volunteered their services to the legitimate fighting forces. Not one American volunteered to serve with Franco's units (Patai, 1995)

The volunteer nurses set up base hospitals, surgical mobile units, field hospitals, and first-aid stations and worked close to the front serving in every major battle (Patai, 1995). A large contingent of nurses (46) came from America and over one-half (28) were "secular" Jews who identified themselves as "humanists, assimilationists, internationalists, and antifascists" (Patai, 1995, pp. 84-85). Many of the volunteers spoke Yiddish and were able to communicate with their Jewish colleagues from other countries. Most of them had strong liberal or leftist leanings, and some were members of the Communist party. They already knew, at that time, that Jews had been targeted as victims of Nazism.

Esther Silverstein Blanc (see Chapter 5), along with other Jewish volunteer nurses, expressed revulsion towards Fascism and its threat to the Jewish people (Patai, 1995). These nurses were social activists, imbued with humanitarian ideals, but the cause that they supported was destined for defeat in Spain. After the war was over, most of them volunteered for and served in the U.S. military in World War II. This did not prevent their being harassed during the "witch-hunts" of the 1950s wherein they were targeted because of their political views. Nevertheless, they remained proud of their work in Spain and continued their activism for social justice (Patai, 1995).

World War II and After

Jubilant over the success of his other military ventures, Hitler, in 1939, attacked Poland and unleashed a new war in Europe. After the Japanese sneak attack on Pearl Harbor at the end of 1941, the United States declared war on Japan. Almost immediately, Germany declared war on the United States, and once again the major countries of the world were in a global conflict, for which America was ill-prepared.

All through the 1930s, the American people had experienced widespread unemployment. Nurses were unable to find jobs, enrollment in nursing schools was declining, and in 1939, only 672 nurses were in the Army Nurse Corps. Over the next 2 years, some measures of preparedness had been launched, so that by December 1941, over 7,000 nurses were in the Army, and a slight increase in enrollment of students in nursing schools was noted (Sarnecky, 1999). However, with the outbreak of hostilities, the nation was suddenly faced with a critical need for nursing staff in military hospitals. A campaign was launched to recruit nurses for the armed forces. In addition, to further stimulate enrollment in nursing schools, the U.S. Cadet Nurse Corps was established under the Bolton Act as a means of encouraging young women to go into nursing.

Before the war came to an end, thousands of nurses had served in the U.S. military. According to one source, more than 75,000 nurses had served—12,239 in the Navy and 62,790 in the Army (Kalisch & Kalisch, 1986). Sarnecky (1999) cites other sources of data that place "the peak strength of the Army Nurse Corps at 55,950 on 31 August 1945" (pp. 278, 476). The U.S. Cadet Nurse Corps, before it was terminated in 1948, had enrolled 179,000 young women (Kalisch & Kalisch, 1986). Serving within the ranks of the Army, Navy, and Cadet Nurse Corps were many Jewish nurses, but we have no information about their number.

In recent years, efforts have been made to seek out Jewish men and women who served their country during World War II and to obtain descriptions of their personal experiences. The National Museum of American Jewish Military History is compiling personal histories, among which are many from Jewish nurses who had served in the military. A cursory review of the first batch of personal histories submitted by these nurses reveals a wide variety of experiences. Most of them were in the Army Nurse Corps; some were in the Navy. They served in the United States, Europe, and the Pacific. Some of them served as flight nurses. In their personal comments they spoke about how proud they were to be serving with the U.S. military forces. They described their admiration and respect for the "wonderful men" they took care of and hoped to be remembered for helping in the war against totalitarianism. They also expressed deep feelings about their patriotism and devotion to duty (Personal histories from the archives of the National Museum of American Jewish Military History).

Individual researchers have undertaken projects such as the one carried out by Debora Duerksen who produced the documentary, *We Were In It Too: American Jewish Women Veterans Remember World War II*. This very moving film points to a substantive presence of Jewish women in the U.S. military during World War

II, and it incorporates an account of the experiences of a Jewish nurse, Lt. Lillian Toll-Tekel. Toll-Tekel, whose final months in the Army Nurse Corps were spent in Germany, described what it meant to be Jewish and a military officer in a position of responsibility with the Army of Occupation. Toll-Tekel also contributed a narrative as one of the respondents to the survey of Jewish nurses described in Chapters 6-9.

The 1999 exhibit *Women in the Military: A Jewish Perspective* at the National Museum of American Jewish Military History featured several Jewish nurses from World War II, as follows:

Ruth Karsevar, in early 1945, was stationed as an Army nurse near the combat zone of Bad Kreuznach, Germany, at the 136th Evacuation Hospital. Here she began to receive many patients from the newly liberated prison camps and concentration camps, and she soon realized the fate that had befallen the Jews of Europe. She often confronted German civilians who worked at her hospital, "always letting them know how proud she was to be an American Jew." (Women in the Military, 1999, p. 22)

Stephanie Markowitz "was the first woman to escape from Nazi occupied territory. Following a plane crash over Albania, Stephanie walked 7 hours a day through knee high snow and raging blizzards, including 5 days without sleep, while successfully dodging German bombing planes. After 60 days on foot, Stephanie reached safety." (Women in the Military, 1999, p. 8)

Miriam Miller joined the Navy Nurse Corps in 1943, and in 1945 she was assigned to a Fleet Hospital in Guam. She was one of the nurses who cared for the heavy casualties of the war in the Pacific. She recalled "the dedication, patriotism, and heroism of Americans willing to sacrifice anything for the ideals we hold so dear—liberty and the pursuit of happiness." (Women in the Military, 1999, p. 19)

Yetta Moskowitz served as a flight nurse with the Army Nurse Corps in the South Pacific. In 1944-45 she participated in operations that evacuated the many casualties fresh from the battlefields straight into the regional area hospitals. She performed bravely under fire and earned a promotion as chief nurse of her squadron. (Women in the Military, 1999, p. 24)

Mildred Scheier was assigned as an Army nurse to a field hospital in Italy in 1943. En route, she survived a German attack on her ship, and she landed safely in North Africa. After a few months, she finally arrived at her base in Italy. One of her fondest memories was when she, as an officer, was asked in the spring of 1944 to lead Passover services for enlisted men in Bari, Italy, where "over 1,000 Jewish boys attended the Seder." (Women in the Military, 1999, p. 23)

Frances Slanger was a Jewish nurse from Roxbury, Mass., to whom special tribute has been paid. (Women in the Military, 1999, p. 26)

Lt. Frances Slanger

Lt. Frances Slanger was the only Army nurse killed by enemy action in the push from Normandy to the Rhine (Sarnecky, 1999). Slanger was one of four nurses who waded ashore at the Normandy beachhead on D-Day. Assigned to the 45th Field Hospital, she was with her platoon near Henri Chapelle (Belgium) on October 21, 1944. Early that morning she lay awake writing a letter to *Stars and Stripes*, the GI newspaper, expressing her profound admiration and respect for the patience, determination, courage, and fortitude of the American GIs. The letter that she was writing was published on November 7, 1944, from which the following passage is quoted:

> It is 0200 and I have been lying awake for one hour, listening to the steady, even breathing of the other three nurses in the tent. We have read several articles in different magazines and papers sent in by a grateful GI, praising the work of the nurses around the combat areas. Praising us—for what? The GIs say we rough it. We in our little tent can't see it. . . . We wade ankle deep in mud. You have to lie in it. We are restricted to our immediate area, a cow pasture or hay field, but then, who is not restricted? We have a stove and coal. We even have a laundry line in the tent... Sure we rough it, but in comparison to the way you men are taking it, we can't complain, nor do we feel that bouquets are due us. But you, the men behind the guns, the men driving our tanks, flying our planes, sailing our ships, building bridges and to the men who pave the way and to the men who are left behind—it is to you we doff our helmets. To every GI wearing the American uniform, for you we have the greatest admi-

Lieutenant Frances Slanger

First American nurse killed by enemy action in the push from Normandy to the Rhine in World War II.
Courtesy of the National Museum of American Jewish Military History

ration and respect. We have learned a great deal about our American soldier and the stuff he is made of. The wounded do not cry. Their buddies come first. The patience and determination they show, the courage and fortitude they have is sometimes awesome to behold. It is a privilege to be able to receive you (Sarnecky, 1999, pp. 239-240).

Several hours later, after she finished writing her letter, Slanger's unit came under an artillery barrage from the enemy, and she was mortally wounded when one of the shells burst nearby. She died 2 hours later and was buried in the American military cemetery of Henri Chapelle. As a memorial to her, an Army hospital ship was named the Frances L. Slanger, making its first voyage in June 1945. In Boston, a library at the former Boston City Hospital bears her name; also, a chapter of the Jewish War Veterans in Boston is named the Lieutenant Frances Slanger Post. The stone marker on her grave bears her name in English and Hebrew, with the following inscription, which was taken from her letter: "The wounded do not cry. Their buddies come first" (Women in the Military, 1999, p. 26). Some years later, Slanger's family had her remains removed and interred in a Jewish cemetery in Roxbury, Mass.

In September 1995, on the 50th anniversary of the formal ceremony marking the end of World War II, a special program was held by the Hadassah Nurses Council of Philadelphia to honor local Jewish nurses who had served in the military. Twenty nurses, most of whom had served in World War II, were honored: Army Nurse Corps—Shirley Cohen, Libby Smigel Elitzky, Sylvia Erlich (flight nurse), Annette Fabrican, Beatrice Feibus, Sara Shapiro Fogel, Florence Hoffman, Minette Knopman, Lillian Litwin, Mildred Ostrow, Pauline Reisner, Joyce Sherman, Sue Spiegel, Lillian Tekel, Esther Weinberg, Sylvia Zubrow; Navy Nurse Corps— Elsie Dion Carroll, Freda Reed; Air Force Nurse Corps—Bonnie Gurian, Elise Stern (On 50th Anniversary of End of World War II, 1996).

The Korean War and Vietnam War
Jewish nurses served with the American armed forces in the Korean War and Vietnam War. As noted earlier, two of the respon-

dents to the survey discussed in Chapters 6-9 served during the Korean War, as did several of the nurses in the group cited above. One nurse, Marita Silverman Bowden, who served in the Vietnam War, shared her experiences in an oral history for the National Museum of American Jewish Military History.

> Marita Silverman Bowden served in the U.S. Army Nurse Corps from 1969-1973. Born in Portsmouth, Va., and raised in Washington, D.C., Bowden studied at the University of Maryland, where she earned the BSN degree in 1966. After graduation she lived and worked in Baltimore, Md. In 1969, she volunteered to serve in the Army Nurse Corps after she realized that "[it] was the peak of the war in Vietnam. . . . I felt I should do my part to take care of the fighting forces. . . . This was not a 'spur of the moment' decision, but rather planned for nearly one year." (Personal history from archives of the National Museum of American Jewish Military History).

Captain Marita Silverman (Bowden)

Lighting the Sabbath candles in Da Nang, South Vietnam, early 1971, probably January or February. Note fatigue uniform. Courtesy of Captain Marita Silverman (Bowden)

In 1970, Bowden was sent to Vietnam where she served for 4 months as Emergency Room Night Supervisor at the Eighth Field Hospital at An Khe. It was a small hospital in an isolated area that daily received numerous casualties. Bowden's primary responsibility was to stabilize the patients for transfer to larger hospitals. When the hospital was closed, Bowden was reassigned to the 95th Evacuation Hospital at Da Nang. She served there for 8 months in the intensive care unit and in the postanesthesia recovery unit, during a period when casualties were extremely heavy. Looking back at this time, Bowden said:

> It was an experience that served me well in my subsequent professional life. I learned to do a lot with a little. I learned compassion when there wasn't anything else to be done. I developed an inner strength that has continued to serve me well (Women in the Military, 1999, p. 32).

Bowden, in her personal memoir, said that while she met other Jewish medical personnel—physicians, dentists, medical service corps officers—she found that "Jewish nurses were a rarity." She attended Friday evening services as often as she could, sometimes necessitating her being transported to the center by helicopter.

> My Judaism became an outlet. . . . For Passover 1971, there was a Seder in Chu Lai. I had to get special permission to leave the hospital compound. I had to arrange for a helicopter to fly me there and arrived at the designated place as the service was going on (Personal history from archives of the National Museum of American Jewish Military History).

Bowden reported that her grandmother had given her a *mezuzah* (i.e., a special symbol of the Jewish faith that is affixed to the doorpost of one's home) as a good luck and safety talisman. "I kept it close to me every day that I spent in Vietnam, either in the pocket of my fatigue uniform or in my ditty bag" (a small drawstring sack). Several of the people with whom Bowden stayed in touch were Jewish friends whom she met during this period when "we were dedicated to our country. . . . We were doing our job... We were good people involved in an extraordinary event" (Personal history from archives of the National Museum of American Jewish Military History; M.S. Bowden, personal communication, July 2000).

Jewish Nurses in Wartime Service in Israel

To round out the account of Jewish nurses in wartime service—lest we forget—we turn now to the role of Jewish nurses in Israel's wars. Let us first briefly examine the development of the nursing profession in Israel. Historically, there were Christian religious orders of nurses—men and women—serving in the "Holy Land" from the time of the Crusades. In the early 1900s up to World War I, a few Jewish nurses went to Palestine to work among the impoverished Jewish population. For instance, Rose Kaplan and Rae Landy (Chapters 4 and 5) were sent from America by Hadassah just before the outbreak of the war to establish a health program, and Selma Maier came from Germany during the war to start a nursing program at the Shaare Zedek Hospital, which was founded by German Jews in 1902. However, the foundation of the nursing profession in Israel today can be traced to the period of the British Mandate in Palestine (Zwanger, 1968; Stockler, 1986).

Up to the period of World War I, Palestine was a part of the Ottoman Empire. During the war, the British forces under General Allenby captured Jerusalem at the end of 1917 and took over the rest of the country by October 1918. In 1922, the League of Nations officially approved the British Mandate over Palestine. With the British Mandate came "order and regulations, among them rules for employment of health workers" (Stockler, 1986, pp. 51-52). Nurses came from Great Britain to work in government hospitals; other nurses began to arrive from Eastern Europe, America, and Germany; some nurses came after having completed studies at the American University in Beirut.

The British Mandate Government favored non-Jewish health care personnel and catered to the Arab population in providing health care. Zwanger points out, "before 1932, the Mandate government did not contribute to the maintenance of Jewish health institutions; it did not recognize any responsibility in this area because the Jewish community had its own extensive system of health" (Zwanger, 1968, p. 26). By the first part of the 20th century, Jewish hospitals had been established in Palestine. The Hadassah Hospital opened a school of nursing, which graduated its first class in 1921 (Bartal & Steiner-Freud, 1999). The Shaare Zedek Hospital started a school of nursing under the direction of

Schwester Selma Maier (Maier, 1973; Stockler, 1986; Zwanger, 1968). The *Kupat Holim* Beilinson School of Nursing was established in 1936 (Zwanger, 1968). Government schools were also started, and other hospitals opened schools as a means of acquiring service personnel. Nonetheless, the numbers of graduates and students were never sufficient (Stockler, 1986; Zwanger, 1968).

Nursing practice in government hospitals, where British nurses had brought their methods, was not unlike the nursing practice in Hadassah Hospital, which was inspired by American models (Stockler, 1986). Variations in nursing functions were noted between rural and urban hospitals in the early years of the Mandate. Anecdotal accounts by individual nurses, some of whom were immigrants from Eastern Europe, working in rural and provincial hospitals, indicated the enormous challenges they faced in the 1930s. Laboring under very primitive conditions, alone and without support, in the midst of hostile neighbors, they found creative ways to provide care to their comrades. Often it was necessary for them to go beyond their nursing functions. Sometimes they had to assume the responsibilities of the physician; at other times, they had to take on menial tasks—fetch and carry water, do the cooking, perform housekeeping chores, and so on. Nonetheless, many were steadfast in their ideals, "In Europe we worked in large modern hospitals, but here was our dream" (Stockler, 1986, p. 58).

As the 1930s drew to a close with the outbreak of World War II, Palestinian Jewish nurses in 1939 were willing to serve in the British Army, but their offer was ignored. When the British ran into serious trouble in 1941-42, after the enemy successes under General Rommel, their need for military medical and nursing personnel was critical. A survey carried out in 1941 indicated that several hundred Jewish registered nurses in Palestine were willing to serve in the military, but they were rebuffed. The British were not willing to accept them as certified, registered nurses. In December 1941, the British established ten types of paramedical positions for Palestinian Jewish women but did not include registered nurses. Ultimately, the Jewish community in Palestine gave up their attempt to persuade the British to accept their nurses into the military forces (Hurwich, 1997).

The next few years witnessed the Allied victory, the end of World War II, the partition of Palestine, the termination of the British Mandate, and the creation of the State of Israel. With the partition of Palestine in 1947 came the outbreak of major hostilities between the Arabs and the Jews. This period marked the beginning of Israel's War of Independence, which continued until a United Nations cease-fire order went into effect in 1949.

As the war got under way, the military authorities in January 1948 called for a survey of Jewish nursing personnel, in preparation for the need to initiate a draft. A repeat survey was carried out in May 1948, upon the establishment of the State of Israel, and the existence of a critical shortage of nurses was confirmed (Hurwich, 1997). According to Hurwich (1997), the number of nurses had declined after the early 1940s because young women of that era were discouraged from entering nursing and were drawn to volunteer army service in other fields. The draft called for nursing candidates from 18 to 45 years of age. Military ranks for nursing personnel were recommended as follows:

Head Nurse—First Lieutenant
Registered Nurse—Second Lieutenant
Practical Nurse—Sergeant

At the end of November 1948, just before the height of the War of Independence, 161 registered nurses and 102 practical nurses were serving in military hospitals (Hurwich, 2000). Thus, the new State of Israel lost no time in nullifying the demeaning practice that the British had adopted toward Jewish nurses even during their darkest hours in World War II. A new pattern for the recognition of nursing in the military was established and maintained in the wars that have occurred throughout the 50-plus years of the modern State of Israel.

Summary

A significant segment of nursing history involves the participation of nurses in wartime service. The need for nurses becomes critical in times of war and other national emergencies, and nurse-historians generally point out that achievements in nursing have often coincided with wars. Nursing history is replete with the description of individual women who served their country as care givers to their sick and wounded military personnel in time of war. And, lest we forget, this chapter presents a general overview of Jewish nurses in wartime service in various countries at different periods of history, and it incorporates brief sketches of individual Jewish nurses who were motivated to respond to a call of duty for reasons of patriotism, personal ideals, or both.

References

American Jewish Military Museum Archives. Oral Histories. Washington, DC.

Bartal, N., & Steiner-Freud, J. (1999). *The first graduating class, Hadassah School of Nursing 1921.* New York: Hadassah, The Women's Zionist Organization of America.

Benson, E. R. (1974). Nursing in Serbia: Early days. *American Journal of Nursing, 74,* 472-474.

Benson, E. R. (1984). A note on Ellen Key's Florence Nightingale and Bertha von Suttner: Two women at war against war. *Cassandra: the Radical Feminist Nurses Newsjournal, 2* (3), 10-12.

Benson, E. R. (1991). The maiden of Kosovo and nursing in Serbia. *IMAGE: Journal of Nursing Scholarship, 23* (1), 57-59.

Benson, E. R. (1992). On the other side of the battle: Russian nurses in the Crimean War. *IMAGE: Journal of Nursing Scholarship, 24* (1), 65-68.

Benson, E. R. (1995). Nursing in Germany: A historical study of the Jewish presence. *Nursing History Review, 3,* 189-200.

Biographical notes on Mathilda Scheuer, RN, president, American Nurses' Association. *Miami Beach, May 6, 1960, Press Release.* Washington, DC: American Nurses' Association.

Chernow, R. (1993). *The Warburgs: The twentieth century odyssey of a remarkable Jewish family (p. 73).* New York: Random House.

Dolan, J. A. (1978). *Nursing in society: A historical perspective* (pp. 176, 186). Philadelphia: Saunders.

Donahue, M. P. (1985). *Nursing: The finest art.* St. Louis: Mosby.

Duerksen, D. (Producer). (2000). *We were in it too: American-Jewish women veterans remember World War II* [Film]. (Available from the producer.)

Hurwich, B. (1997). We are all on the front lines: The pre-state years: 1911-1947. *Military medicine in Israel, Part I* (In Hebrew). Tel Aviv, Israel: Government of Israel Ministry of Defence Printing Office.

Hurwich, B. (2000). The fifth front: The Israeli soldier (the Medical Service of the "Hagana" and of the Israel Defence Forces [IDF] during the War of Independence, 1947-1949). *Military medicine in Israel, Part II* (In Hebrew). Tel Aviv, Israel: Government of Israel Ministry of Defence Printing Office.

Kalisch, P. A., & Kalisch, B. J. (1986). *The advance of American nursing* (2nd ed.). Boston: Little, Brown.

Kaplan, M. A. (1991). *The making of the Jewish middle class: Women, family, and identity in imperial Germany.* New York: Oxford University Press.

Key, E. (1919). *Florence Nightingale und Bertha von Suttner, zwei Frauen im Kriege wider den Krieg.* Zurich: M. Rascher.

Maier, S. (1973). *My life and experiences at "Shaare Zedek."* Jerusalem: Shaare Zedek Hospital.

Mayer, S. (1997). Naomi Deutsch. In P. E. Hyman & D. D. Moore, *Jewish women in America: A historical encyclopedia.* New York: Routledge.

Natalija - Neti Munk: Povodom 50 - godisnjice smrti. (1974, maj-juni). *Jevrejski Pregled,* br. 5-6, str. 68-69. [Nettie Munk: On the 50th anniversary of her death. (1974, May-June). *Jewish Review,* 5-6, pp. 68-69.] Beograd [Belgrade], Yugoslavia.

On 50th anniversary of the end of World War II. (1996, Spring). *Nursing: The Jewish Connection.* Hadassah National Center for Nurses Councils Newsletter, p. 10.

Patai, F. (1995). Heroines of the good fight: Testimonies of U.S. volunteer nurses in the Spanish Civil War, 1936-1939. *Nursing History Review, 3,* 79-104.

Sarnecky, M. T. (1997). Nursing in the American Army from the revolution to the Spanish-American War. *Nursing History Review, 5,* 49-69.

Sarnecky, M. T. (1999). *A history of the U.S. Army Nurse Corps.* Philadelphia: University of Pennsylvania Press.

Stockler, R. A. (1986). *Hospital nursing in the Holy Land from the period of the Crusades to the first five years of the State of Israel.* Tel Aviv, Israel: Tel Aviv University, Department of Nursing.